Leave Your Nose Ring at Home

GET THE JOB YOU WANT BY CREATING A POWERFUL FIRST IMPRESSION

By Joe Swinger

Foreword by Ron Fry

CAREER PRESS

Franklin Lakes, NJ

LEAVE YOUR NOSE RING AT HOME
EDITED AND TYPESET BY CHRISTOPHER CAROLEI
Cover design by Lu Rossman/Digi Dog Design NYC
Printed in the U.S.A. by Book-mart Press

To order this title, please call toll-free 1-800-CAREER-1 (NJ and Canada: 201-848-0310) to order using VISA or MasterCard, or for further information on books from Career Press.

The Career Press, Inc., 3 Tice Road, PO Box 687,
Franklin Lakes, NJ 07417
www.careerpress.com

Library of Congress Cataloging-in-Publication Data

Swinger, Joe, 1954-
    Leave your nose ring at home : get the job you want by creating a powerful first impression / by Joe Swinger.
        p. cm.
    Includes index.
    ISBN-13: 978-156414-875-9
    ISBN-10: 1-56414-875-0 (paper)
        1. Job hunting. 2. Impression formatting (Psychology) I. Title.

HF5382.7.S95 20006
650.1--dc22

2006043918

Dedication

To Sandy, for her love and belief.
To Jonathan and Kevin, for their smiles and laughter.
To Casey and Ruth, for their gift of life.

Dedication

Acknowledgments

There are many people to thank for helping make *Leave Your Nose Ring at Home* a reality. My wife, Sandy, who has been with me every step of the way for nearly 20 years. Thank you for your patience and understanding during the writing process. I don't know how I could have done it without you.

Jonathan and Kevin, for keeping things light with their smiles and laughter. I know it was extremely difficult to always hear that I had no time to play!

Career Press and Ron Fry for believing in this project from the very beginning. Michael Pye for his willingness to listen to my questions and ideas. Chris Carolei for his insightful editing.

My family, Elaine Rolke, John Swinger, Joanne Perone, Michael Swinger, and Barbara Pondo, for offering feedback and being as excited about the book as I was.

Casimir Swinger, M.D., for his insightful critiques and suggestions during our many long, sleepless nights. G. would be proud of you!

Rick Williams for always being there to listen to my dreams.

The EMI team of Kurt Mortensen, Joycebelle Edlebrock, and Denise Michaels for their help in the creation and development of the book idea and proposal.

Mark Victor Hansen and Robert G. Allen for helping to make my dream come true.

I also want to thank everyone I have ever worked with at Circuit City who has contributed to my development both as an interviewer and as a manager. Jerry Mabbott for being one of the best managers and friends I have ever been fortunate to have. John Johnston for his encouragement, feedback, and promotion on my behalf. Scott Ebner for allowing me the time off to complete my manuscript.

The great Rocky Mountain Regional team for always being there when I needed them.

Thank you Lew Woolford, Mike Blackburn, and Brian Taylor for contributing their interviewing stories, Carli Katis for assisting me with the book's marketing and promotion, and Brian Done for being the Webmaster who got the whole thing started.

To my team at Jordan Landing, where this book idea was conceived, you make my job fun and cause me to learn something new about myself every day—you guys rock!

Thank you Sue Cano, John Cluff, Stephanie Holfeltz, and Brandon Lystrup for your encouragement, feedback, and support while I was away from the store writing, and for keeping the PMI high!

Lastly, I would like to thank the thousands of applicants I have interviewed in my retail career. This book is both because of you and for you. I hope that I somehow affected you just as much as you affected me.

—Joe Swinger

Contents

Foreword

Leave your nose ring at home! And your bangles and beads and cloying perfume and flip-flops and bad attitude and complaints. Why? So you can get the job!

Don't be scared, but Joe Swinger will challenge you right from the git-go. As he writes in his Introduction, "What's holding you back from getting the job you want? Look in the mirror after a day of job searching. Does a powerful first impression stare back at you? Would you hire yourself in the first few minutes?

"Are you wearing a smile or a frown? Does the light dance off your facial piercings? Are you dressed for business or for hanging out? If you shook hands with your image would you gross yourself out? Do you get tired just looking at your low level of energy?"

Leave Your Nose Ring at Home is *not* a book about grooming, about how to write the perfect resume, or even about how to get a job, although it talks about all those topics and many more. It *is* about how to go about creating a powerful, energetic, passionate first impression, one that will not only get you a job, but probably help you succeed at it as well.

I can almost hear your disbelief. Okay, you probably agree that creating a good first impression is a smart move, maybe even an essential one in certain situations. But a *key* (*the* key) to getting a job? *Nah.*

Sorry, but as Joe will convince you, making a powerful first impression on an enlightened hiring manager may be a major qualification for the job in and of itself. And it can certainly be the difference between you and that other candidate who seems to have a similar education, the same experience, and the same skills as you.

My favorite "first impression" story involves a football quarterback (He Who Shall Not be Named) who was supposed to be the New York Jets' top draft pick some years ago. He, the General Manager, and his wife had a nice and uneventful dinner at a local restaurant. When they left, it was unexpectedly raining. Only the quarterback had an umbrella. While hurling a quick "goodbye and thanks" over his shoulder, he sprinted for his own car, leaving his hosts to slog through the rain.

As a result, the second quarterback on the draft board was chosen instead. His name was Joe Namath. And the other quarterback? He probably never even guessed what had soured the Jets.

You certainly don't have to be a top college quarterback to blow your chances with an interviewer without even knowing it. Many interviewers actually start interviewing in the reception area, asking seemingly innocuous questions such as,

"How are you doing?", "How was your flight?", or "Did you have any trouble finding us?" You would probably be surprised to hear of the numerous candidates who thought these and similar questions were opportunities to complain about their lives, the weather, the flight, the directions, and much, much more. It would probably not (and certainly shouldn't) surprise you to know that the vast majority of these candidates were dismissed while still in the reception area!

Joe is not a career counselor, headhunter, or professional resume writer. He is someone who *hires people every day*, one of those "enlightened" managers who has learned to value competencies over experience. As a result, he often finds himself waving goodbye to candidates who seemed perfect for the position, in favor of others who lacked many of the specific qualifications for the job. But the latter have one thing in common: They made an indelible first impression on Joe.

Are you ready to make such an impression? *Leave Your Nose Ring at Home* will show you how, step by step, smile by smile. Wouldn't it be great to beat out a better-qualified candidate, to land a job you knew was a stretch? Learn Joe's secrets and you invariably will!

—Ron Fry

It Only Takes a Moment to Change Your Life:

Change Yours Today

Warning! The reading of this book is dangerous to your current state of mental health! If you currently believe that whatever happens in your life is outside of your control, you will soon begin to experience life on *your* terms.

If you currently believe that you cannot get the job you want because of your poor work history or your troubled past, you will begin to get the jobs the others can't. If your personality lets you down when you need it most—during the interview—you will become a confident, energetic applicant who will be able to get the job you want within minutes.

Why This Book

The book you hold in your hands is nothing more than the result of failure. Thousands of failures. Each dream that was squashed—each house that was lost, each marriage that ended—resulted from the fact that I turned down an applicant rather than give him or her a job.

As someone who has been trained in the helping profession, it has always been difficult for me to turn an applicant down for a job. I see the people I interview every day as more than just another needed exercise for me to staff my store. Each individual who steps into my office has needs to fill and dreams he or she hopes to achieve. Perhaps he or she desperately needs money to maintain a home, feed a family, or pay for schooling. Perhaps he or she dreams of getting a job with my company in the hope of making a career of it.

As the hiring manager in my store, I am put in the unenviable position of being the person who either grants wishes or squashes hopes. It is not something that I take lightly. Nothing would please me more than to give everyone who needed a job a place for them to utilize their skills and talents, and hopefully reach their dreams.

However, it is not to be. Business today demands productive associates who can contribute across a variety of levels. Business today requires associates who can excel despite the stresses of the service industry—who are where they are because they want to be and not because they have to be.

My Fantasy

It was about a year ago that something changed. It got to the point where I was turning down so many applicants that I began to wonder why. Were my standards too high? And, if they were, what were those standards, and could they be articulated?

I noticed that I looked for the same attributes that appeared to give me and my management team the greatest successes in our store. The same attributes that allowed my associates to succeed and move up into management.

I often wished that I could step out of my character as Store Director and meet with the applicant outside for several minutes before the interview, to tell him or her exactly what I was looking for, and what he or she needed to do to get the job.

Sometimes I would be in an interview with an applicant who I really wanted to see get the job and think, "If only he would have done this, said that, and acted this way, then I would have been able to hire him." It all seemed so easy to me.

I began to wonder, what if I could teach the applicants before they go on an interview exactly what they would need to do to ensure success? What if I could give them the tools and the service industry insider secrets necessary for them to get the job they wanted?

The Secret Key

After a year of complaining to my team that someone should write a book to give the applicants the straight story and help them get the job they wanted, I decided to write it myself. However, the last thing I felt the world needed was another tiresome book on how to write the perfect resume, or how to correctly answer 150 interview questions.

What I wanted to offer was a key—a secret key—that would allow my readers to create such a powerful first impression

that you would be able to get the job you wanted within minutes. A secret key that I had created not just from the experiences of more than a thousand interviews, but from my
own personal failures and successes. A system so powerful
that, when you had finished reading the book, you could literally use the knowledge gained to unlock the door to the
job you wanted and enter the other side as a valued, productive associate.

I believe I have created it and you are now holding it in
your hands.

Change Your Life Today

Decide today to change your life once and for all, and live
your life on your terms and not someone else's. This book will
show you how to create a positive, digital mind so that you will
no longer have your energy and time dissipated by your negative, analog thinking. It will show you how to identify and ac-
quire the necessary attributes to create your own powerful
first impression so you will be able to get the job you want—
and achieve your dreams.

I believe I have given you the blueprint that will not only
help you get the job you want, but also help you build a new
and better life. Now it is up to you to do the necessary work
to lay the foundation that will stay with you throughout your
entire life.

I'm going to show you how to quickly get the entry-level
service industry job you want by creating such a powerful first
impression that you will transform into an applicant who will
be able to confidently enter any interview armed with the
knowledge that the job is yours.

I'll hook you up with the latest psychological principles geared to capturing the interviewer in the first few minutes. You'll lose your outdated, analog thinking on the inside, and learn to think in a clear, digital manner that programs you for success so your powerful first impression sings on the outside.

We'll work together on separating you from the stereotypical, entitlement-generation applicants, and grabbing the jobs the others can't. Now is the absolute best time to get your first job or change markets, and capturing a job outside your comfort zone won't be a problem after you discover where the schools of hungry fish are.

You'll no longer be wondering if you have the "look" for the role you're auditioning for after you discover how to make yourself indispensable to any hiring manager by focusing on the 20 percent of the attributes that will contribute 80 percent of the productivity.

Using This Book

I am now seeing job search books numbering near 500 pages! Is this what it has come to for one to get a decent job? Judging by the career section in book stores, it appears that it is now harder to become employed than it is to get a part in a sitcom. If you're similar to most busy young adults, you don't have the time or the desire to wade through a bunch of pages in the hope that you'll gain some nugget of information that will help you get a job. The good news is that you don't have to.

I am not a career counselor. I give people the job they want as a part of my daily responsibilities, and I give it to them quickly. I am not going to feed you information that I dreamed up in my office that I think might work. I am going to give you the straight answers so you too can get the job you want, be able to pay your bills, and begin working on your dreams.

A service-industry job is absolutely the easiest to get, and I've done my best to point out the important facts that will get you both the interview and the job in the shortest amount of time possible. I've strategically placed helpful action and informational items such as *Real Life* and *Joe's Gem* to replace long-winded case studies, so you can get the interview or job you want and move on with life. After all, we both know there are more important things to do!

This book is not a "nuts and bolts" type of book. This book examines what it takes to create a powerful first impression because, no matter what the experts differ on, I believe most would agree that this is a "people" business. Yes, I hire associates with the right competencies and intangibles, but more importantly, I hire people.

I hire associates that I believe will "fit in" with the team and will bring a sense of fun to the workplace, in addition to achieving results. Thus, every chapter in the book is geared towards creating a powerful first impression that will help you get the job you want within minutes.

The book is written towards the service industry, but with an emphasis on the retail and food trades. (Retail and food workers are some of the hardest-working, but lowest-paid employees in the service industry. Yet, these associates are responsible for most front-line customer service and sales revenues). However, the information in this book can apply to any entry-level job in the service industry.

Open Your Mind

You will be required to read this book with an open mind because this is precisely what we will be doing—opening your mind! Opening your mind to the job you want, to the intangible qualities you need, and to the goals you want to achieve.

This isn't a career book for you to discover what you want to do—but rather one for you to discover who you want to be and how you want to think of yourself in your career. This will not be a lab assignment. This will be a field study in behavior—yours!

You will be asked to answer a few questions about how you think, as well as recognize and observe certain behaviors of both yourself and others while doing your normal routine of school, shopping, and recreation.

If this book helps you in getting the service industry job you want, then I will have done my job. If this book also helps you become a more focused individual who can clearly see your future and have the confidence and passion to get there, then you will have done yours.

And please remember: I'm here to help. If you need additional help, please feel free to visit me on the Web at *joeswinger.com*. I plan on supplying a list of frequently asked questions for your review, as well as a reader message board where everyone will be able to assist each other with ideas, interviewing tips, and real-life job issues. You can also write me at *nosering@joeswinger.com* at any time and I will do my best to personally answer any of your job questions. I also look forward to any suggestions you may have for future editions of this book.

Chapter 1

Be Who You Are:

Create Your Own Powerful First Impression

The actor received a standing ovation as he thanked those in the industry for helping him receive the best-actor award. He could feel the statue in his hand as he rubbed his fingers over it. Suddenly, a coworker grabbed him by his shoulder and told him that his break was over, and it was time to go back to waiting tables.

I began the writing of this book just days before the disastrous destruction of Hurricane Katrina in New Orleans and the gulf region. At the time it was little more than an unfortunate diversion that allowed me to procrastinate and watch the horror on television. It was one of those events that I tend to watch for hours and then get burned out with a case of *CNN*

21

overdose, which meant that it was time to go back to my writing. Little did I know that I would later get personally involved.

My employer, Circuit City, had several stores shut down there for an extended period due to the storm. It was many days before the company was even sure if all its associates were safe. After several weeks, a few stores were opened with minimal staffing. Customer traffic, fresh with Federal Emergency Management Agency (FEMA) and Red Cross money, was beyond what one sees at any Christmas season. I was asked to go to New Orleans and lend managerial support.

I was put in charge of hiring associates to help with the increased traffic. I silently wondered to myself on the plane ride from Salt Lake City whether or not the same rules of a powerful first impression applied to the citizens of New Orleans. The doubt that filled my mind was so strong that it caused me to temporarily forget my fear of flying.

Frankly, after several nights of watching *CNN*, I anticipated interviewing only the poor, uneducated, minority applicants portrayed on the television. Was it actually possible for one of them to get the job they wanted—within just a few minutes—by creating a powerful first impression? Or were the principles in my book just a figment of my race, education, and opportunity?

The questions continued to run through my head as I left my temporary office to greet the first applicant. How was she going to be, and what would her impact be on my beliefs? My questions were answered within minutes.

I was greeted by what seemed to be one of the biggest, most engaging smiles I had ever seen. The young African-American woman was nicely dressed, but she still apologized that all her clothes were lost in the flood and this was all she had. I knew at that moment I just had to hire her. Despite a situation where she could have begged for a job becuase her previous employer was out of business, she eloquently stated why she wanted to work for Circuit City, and why she would be a benefit to the company.

This scene would play out again and again throughout the next several days. Applicants, many of whom were displaced from nursing and information technology programs at New Orleans and Tulane universities, would win me over in minutes with their fortitude and willingness to change their lives due to the catastrophic event. Applicants, who lost their homes and businesses and had every right to be angry with the world, would confidently state why they were perfect for the position (even though they didn't have a whit of retail experience).

I hired nearly 20 associates during that period, all of whom I wished I could have put on the plane with me and taken back to Salt Lake City. I was truly blessed to have been a part of such an extraordinary experience. As I reflected back on my time in New Orleans, I realized that the power of a first impression is universal, and race, education, and opportunity play no role in it—and what an empowering moment that was!

What's Your Excuse?

What's holding *you* back from getting the job you want? Are you using a "catastrophe" in your life to sabotage your interviews, or are you more similar the "New Orleans Twenty" who decided to create a powerful first impression despite theirs? Look in the mirror after a day of job searching. Does a powerful first impression stare back at you when you first glance at the image? Would you hire yourself in the first few minutes? Are you wearing a smile or a frown? Does the light dance off your facial piercings? Are you dressed for business or for hanging out? If you shook hands with your image would you gross yourself out? Do you get tired just looking at your low level of energy?

Warm Body Syndrome

This book began as a simple response to a habitual problem I have as a Circuit City Store Director. Namely, how can I fill my store with qualified associates who possess the intangible attributes needed to perform at a consistent high level of productivity? It is imperative in such a high-turnover industry as mine to find an associate pipeline that will enable me to continually hire top talent, similar to a perennial college football powerhouse that must combat graduation and early departures to the National Football League (NFL).

It was evident after thousands of interviews with "qualified" applicants that something was missing. I would hire associates with technology or entertainment sales backgrounds and they would fail miserably. They never seemed to "get it" regarding customer engagement. Sometimes they would have high-volume months, but always at the cost of quality. Customer-service associates always seemed to lack the drive and desire to do whatever was necessary to create a memorable experience for the customer.

I would sometimes spend 30 minutes with applicants in the hope they would say something at the end to justify my hiring them to help staff my departments, oftentimes asking loads of computer-generated questions created specifically for the applicant by our workforce staffing company. Why?

Shock Treatment

It took Rosa, a Hispanic waitress, to awaken me to my senses. Needing associates for a new store I was opening, I went against all reason for hiring a waitress and interviewed her. Talk about a powerful first impression! Her smile and energy were so contagious that I knew within the first few minutes that I was going to hire her. This time I also talked for 30 minutes, but only because she was so enjoyable.

I sized her up as we chatted, continually trying to assess where to put her. She obviously understood add-on sales because she had sold appetizers, desserts, and drinks. Would she be able to convert that talent to add-on computer software, peripherals, and extended warranties?

I'm ashamed to admit that I quickly discounted the idea that a waitress could be successful in a computer-technology department, so I placed her in the safer customer-service environment. It took less than a week after seeing her skills at work to realize I had made a mistake.

I immediately repositioned Rosa in the technology department, where she developed into a management candidate and one of the top performers in the store, winning many associate of the month awards, and, yes, oftentimes leading the department in add-on sales.

One hire led to many others, including more waitresses and fast-food workers, a physical therapist, construction and call-center workers, and many, many teens with no job experience. My management team and I turned convention on its ear and developed a team that consistently produced results in addition to continually being ranked near the top of the company in customer service. We also cranked out the management candidates who would go on to become top per-formers at other stores.

How did we do it? By hiring competencies rather than experience, and exploiting the powerful first impression method that allowed us to decide within minutes whether or not to offer the job.

After much heartache and the turning down of numerous applicants who just could not get past the first few minutes, I asked myself why intelligent people would sabotage their op-portunity by creating a weak first impression. Why would the vast majority reply with the same poor answers, wear the same inappropriate clothing, and greet me with the same lack of the intangibles needed to become successful?

What Role Are You Auditioning For?

I have spent many years writing screenplays in the trenches of the Hollywood film community, and if it has taught me one thing, it is that one must be prepared and ready with a brilliant writing sample for any fortuitous meeting with a major player or talent.

Similarly, ask any actor how he and she prepares for win-ning a part in a play or film and you will probably receive a litany of answers, because no actor auditions without first knowing the answers to several questions. What character would she play and what is the time period it takes place in? Is there a certain age or look required for the character she is auditioning for? What is the dramatic arc of both the story and the character, and the emotional range required to pull it off? Is there a certain vocal presence that is needed?

You must also be prepared. You will not get the job if you arrive at an interview ready to play a character on *Friends* when the interviewer is looking for Hamlet. You'll never get to sing a note if you arrive prepared to sing the falsetto of the Bee Gees and the role requires the coolness of Usher.

Actors have only a short time during the audition to prove their mettle. It is no secret that casting directors make their decision within minutes. Does the actor have the "look" that the director is looking for? Is she charismatic? Does she have the required energy level and emotional range to carry it off?

Get the Job You Want

Getting the job you want as a young adult is not always about making money and moving up in a company. It's about being able to pay for your rent, buy your groceries, and still have money left over for the enjoyable things in life. It's about having a job that's fun, but challenging. It's about having a job that allows you to pay your bills, but still allows you to pursue your dreams.

Getting the job you want is instrumental in getting the life you want. Whether you aspire to be an actor, a company CEO, an attorney, or a doctor, you may feel that the job you are applying for is nothing special. That perhaps it is beneath what you are capable of doing. Maybe it is a customer-service position dealing with irate people. Maybe you will be making coffee, sweeping floors, or washing dishes.

Whatever job you get, remember that it will allow you to pursue your passions and your dreams. You will get the job you want by creating a powerful first impression but, more importantly, you will also get the means to reach your goals, your dreams—and isn't this what it's really all about?

Maybe you're looking for your first job and you get that "deer in the headlight" look every time you get into an interview. Perhaps you have had a few jobs that you've quit every three months and don't really know what to say when asked about your commitment. Not to worry—we have all been there.

It's Showtime

Many young adults would love to be the next American Idol and get that overnight record deal. But your chance of meeting the interviewer's version of Simon, Paula, and Randy are pretty slim. Closer to the truth is that you'll never get past the gatekeepers to reach the decision-makers.

Actors sometimes spend years learning their craft and then many, many hours rehearsing their role in an attempt to shine during their few minutes in front of the casting director, just to have a chance at their 15 minutes of fame.

You don't have years to get ready for your audition. Maybe you hate your job and just want to get out—anywhere. Maybe you're just punching a clock and want something that stretches your talents. Maybe you're attending school and just want a few extra bucks to splurge on the weekend. Or, unfortunately, maybe you're just broke and need a job today to pay the rent tomorrow.

Whatever your situation, your answer lies inside this book. Wherever you are failing, we'll work on it together. I guarantee that if you follow what has worked for the hundreds of applicants who have come before you, you too will get the job you want by creating a powerful first impression.

Chapter 2

The Thrill of Victory
or the Agony of Defeat:

Get the Job You Want
in Minutes

*The actor knows he is up against insurmountable odds but contin-
ues on believing that someone—somewhere—will see his passion
and believe, as he does, that he has what it takes to be a star.*

In some industries, getting hired is similar to being re-
cruited by a big-time college football team. The college needs
to fill a certain position and it wants to get the best athlete
available to fill it. It looks at many candidates, check out their
resumes (game films), test their speed and ability, and even
bring them on campus to interview them and have them meet
with some of the coaches.

However, top prospects all have the required competencies to succeed at the college level. Sometimes all the charts, film, ability, and interviews do not point to a defined candidate. At that time, the decision as to which player can make the greatest impact on the team, and to whom to offer a scholarship to, becomes nothing more than a gut instinct that the head coach must take a chance on.

Job Interviewing Today

There are many interview techniques and assessment tools available to hiring managers today. Behavioral testing, stress and team interviews, background checks, drug tests, competency assessments, and that holy grail of the job search, the need to have the perfect resume.

But, despite the aforementioned tools of the trade, top-prospect applicants sometimes resemble football recruits in that all have the powerful first impression, the perfect resume, and the perfect answers to the 20 behavioral questions.

As much as some hiring managers are reluctant to say, why one applicant gets the job and another doesn't is sometimes no more psychological than a gut instinct about which candidate is going to be a better team player and perform more successfully with the right coaching.

The Service Industry

The service industry is similar to a small-school football team in that there are fewer top-prospect applicants to compete for the jobs, as well as more openings available. Thus, the opportunities to get the job you want are much greater here than in any other industry.

If you are striking out and not getting hired, there may be several reasons why you cannot get a job in today's market. Perhaps you have limited or no experience. Maybe you are having trouble getting past the gatekeepers and are not being interviewed by those with the power to make the decision.

Perhaps you sometimes have trouble presenting yourself to hiring managers in a convincing enough manner that they believe you have what it takes to do the job. It could be that you are a "free spirit" and interview as someone who is a "flight risk" and will leave the company after a short time.

I believe you can only arrive at the correct reason why by honestly answering a few questions. Why should anyone hire you? Why would anyone hire you? Would you hire yourself? Would you put your reputation, your family, your future on the line if you knew it depended on your performance, as you are asking the hiring manager to do? Would you waste your precious time exploring your background, your strengths, and your weaknesses if you knew that there was possibly another candidate in an interview right after yours that will knock the interviewer's socks off, an applicant who will have the interviewer dying to hire him or her even in the face of conflicting evidence? An applicant who will cause the hiring manager to even put them into a position they have no experience with.

If you answered no to the previous questions, and could not find a reason to even hire yourself, you should be worried. Unless you want to work for a company that hires only temporaries or warm bodies, you are in trouble. Big trouble.

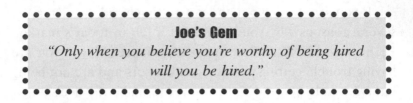

Joe's Gem
"Only when you believe you're worthy of being hired will you be hired."

But all is not lost. *You* can change. *You* can decide now, in the next few minutes, that from this point in your life you are going to be the one who gets the job—even one you're not now qualified to get. Sound too good to be true? Read on.

Real Life

I arrived for my interview with Judy, an applicant for a customer-service position, only to see her anxiously pacing back and forth, as if on guard duty, in front of the customer-service counter. "Is this going to take long? I have my bowling league in a half hour," she said. She was out within minutes. I never heard if she bowled a 300 game!

I admit it. I'm a hiring junkie. Few things give me greater pleasure than discovering a talented applicant who will take a facet of my business to another level. It doesn't matter if I'm interviewing for customer service, sales, or the warehouse. It's getting so difficult to hire associates who can make a difference, that when one is found it can make my week.

As a Store Director for Circuit City, the pressure to find exceptional associates before the competition does is so intense that I perform every first interview in the store for fear a great potential candidate might be turned down by a subordinate manager. This is good news for you. Impress me and you have a job on the spot within minutes.

Hiring Epidemic

A new epidemic is affecting teens across the nation in their ability to get the necessary job experience to carry them throughout their careers. The latest studies show that teen unemployment is rising from increased competition and that the number of working teens aged 16–19 is down 45 percent from five years ago, and it is at its lowest level since 1947. Entry-level jobs that once routinely went to young people are now being given to older people and immigrants due to the maturity levels, dependability, work ethic, and abilities to work as a team often exhibited by these groups.

Older people and immigrants? Can this be true? Does this bother you as much as it bothers me? Isn't it written somewhere in stone that every teen is guaranteed a job as a grocery bagger at Albertsons or flipping burgers at McDonalds? That there's a natural progression from selling lemonade on a corner, to cutting grass, to asking which of the 31 flavors and how many scoops of it one wants?

Today's Generation

Generations are similar to hurricanes: Every one needs a name. We have Baby Boomers and Slackers, Generation X and Generation Y. The current generation of teens is often called the Entitlement Generation because they want the benefits of a corporate veteran on the date of hire. Part-time associates today want two weeks off during the course of a three-month summer employment stint. Young people list coming to work on time as a strength, as if arriving late was an option.

The employer revolt has begun, and it is a buyer's market. Whatever you're selling, you have minutes to do it. After that, you've lost my interest. Whatever you say after that doesn't matter—my mind has already drifted to what I'm going to do after you're out the door.

Sounds brutal? You'd better believe it. Management today is regularly overworked, squeezes in interviews between putting out fires, and is looking for anyone who can fill their basic needs. The good news is that the service-industry job is absolutely the easiest job to get.

Failure Is not an Option

I am going to help you get to wherever you want to go. If you are striking out and not getting hired, I'm going to show you exactly what to do so that you'll be on the payroll in no time. Even better, the skills you learn will serve you in many areas of your life for many years to come.

But, I need your help. I need you to not only follow the advice in this book, but to also believe that failure is not an option. Because it truly isn't.

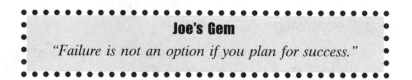

Joe's Gem

"Failure is not an option if you plan for success."

Why should you believe me? Because I have done thousands of interviews and have distilled the process of being hired in the service industry down to the basics. Now is absolutely the best time to be looking for one's first job due to several key industry dynamics in effect. You will learn what these are and how to use them to your benefit. You will discover the many opportunities available because more jobs are now driven by skill-set competencies, rather than specific experience.

Get Ready for Your Audition

Your first job interview is nothing more than preparing for an audition. Similar to a stage and screen actor, there is a certain amount of talent, training, and acting needed to win the role. Few actors enjoy reading cold, for it is difficult to know the character's situation and motivations.

You will win the role you desire to play by knowing your goal, identifying your talent, training yourself to recognize your strengths and opportunities, and, yes, even learning a little bit about acting.

All great acting begins with the development of character. Let's get started on your most famous role: *you!*

First Impressions

Have you ever been in the middle of an interview and silently wondered how things were going? Wondered if you were still being considered for the job—or if you had already blown it? How would you feel if you knew that decision was made in the first few minutes?

Webster defines impression as "an effect produced, as on the mind or senses, by some force or influence." What effect are you having on others? You both create and receive thousands of impressions on a daily basis. Have you ever really examined just what your impressions are saying about you as a person? What are people discovering about you from the way you talk, your gestures, your facial expression, and your tone of voice?

A first impression, depending on the situation, could be any amount of time, from those first few moments, to possibly an hour or more. We have all had teachers who, from the moment they walked into the classroom on the first day of class, you took an immediate dislike to, and you just *knew* it was going to be a difficult year or semester. You have also probably had other teachers that came in as meek as a lamb and you knew the course was cake.

Unfortunately, it's the negative first impressions that I usually remember when it comes to school! When I was attending college for my MBA, I had what appeared to be an extremely unhappy economics professor named Delores. Delores was held in very high esteem at the college and reportedly did very good work.

However, my memory of her is when she stormed into the classroom on our first day, dropped several boxes of books and files on her desk, and then promptly started writing economic theory formulas on the whiteboard. I still remember looking at my neighbor in the seat next to me with a "we're screwed" look.

I'll admit that economics and mathematical theories are not my strengths, but my fear greatly increased when Delores began passing out the syllabus and mentioned that we were already behind in the class. It was our first day! The last straw was her comment that if we were to miss one session of class, we would drop to a "B" and it would go down from there.

I was working at Circuit City as an Operations Manager at the time and knew that I would probably miss a day or two because the semester would run into the busy Christmas season. Naturally, being terrified, I dropped the class the next day!

I guess the case could be made that Delores had a powerful first impression—it just wasn't the one I was looking for. I took it as negative, but there were others in the class who stayed through the semester (maybe because they had to) and may have seen it as positive.

I wonder, looking back at the event, what would have happened had Delores come into the room in a different manner. What if she arrived utilizing a more friendly, engaging style? I probably would have stayed in the course, and who knows what I could have learned from her. Perhaps I would now be an expert in economic theory!

Your First Impressions

Think back to your own powerful first impressions that you have experienced in your life. Who left such a powerful first impression on you that it stills registers in your mind? Maybe it was your spouse's father when you met him for the first time. Perhaps it was the first time you met a high school teacher who ended up becoming one of your mentors. Maybe it was one of your early managers who made an impact on you about what it takes to be a great employee.

Would you consider your recollections negative or positive and why? What was it about the event that affected you the way it did?

A powerful first impression also does not have to be from a person. One can journey to a foreign country and experience an immediate life-changing effect because of the culture's impact. One can also have a powerful first impression walking into an exceptionally beautiful house or hotel—the kind where you can almost smell the money.

You experience fresh impressions all of the time, although they are not on the same level as a powerful first impression, and perhaps not even noticed. When they happen, we have internal conversations with ourselves that will label the event because we will experience some reaction in the first few minutes of meeting someone or encountering a situation:

- **A celebrity.** "He really looks like a phony, although he pretends to care about the environment."

- **Your new car mechanic.** "I don't really know if I can trust him, because he looks so suspicious."

- **A new coworker.** "She looks like the type that will probably try to sleep her way to the top."

- **A new supervisor at work.** "He looks like a workaholic. Looks like I'm going to have to get my act together."

- **A member of the opposite sex.** "He is really cute and has been eyeing me. I wonder if he would like to go to the new movie?"

- **Eating at a restaurant for the first time with a group of friends.** "This place really looks expensive—I wonder if I can afford it?"

The moment we make our decision based on these internal dialogues, we have just judged the impression of that person or event—right or wrong—in a terribly short amount of time.

Sometimes we discover that our first impressions were wrong, but oftentimes not.

First Impression Validation

Many studies have shown that lasting impressions can be formed within minutes of meeting someone. One such study demonstrated that observers, based on 30 seconds of behavior, were amazingly able to predict a teacher's average student-assessment rating at the end of the semester.

Another study has shown that people do seem to arrive at similar first impressions of a person they have not met, even if they have never interacted with him or her.

There is also good evidence that interviewers have trouble changing their initial impressions of a job applicant simply due to the mental demands of interviewing. The simple act of thinking up what questions to ask can impair one's judgment to react to conflicting evidence during the interview.

These results suggest that the simple act of conducting a job interview can place such stress on one's attention span that it can affect an interviewer's impression of job candidates. This is of utmost importance to you in the interview because you will have an extremely short amount of time to make a powerful first impression.

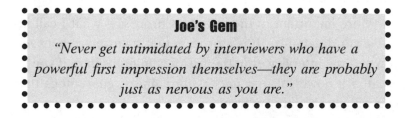

Joe's Gem

"Never get intimidated by interviewers who have a powerful first impression themselves—they are probably just as nervous as you are."

Buyer's Remorse

Cognitive dissonance, proposed by psychologist Leon Festinger in 1957, is the mental discomfort that is caused when a person performs an action that he or she does not believe in. Though it's good to know the psychological term, you can think of it as a form of buyer's remorse.

Are you the type of shopper who has to know the store's return policy because you change your mind often? Chances are you may have had some experience with buyer's remorse at one time or another after you purchased a product, only to begin questioning your decision once the purchase had been made. Perhaps it was another pair of shoes that is just taking space in your closet. You probably discovered that you either had to return the shoes to the store, or create a reason to keep them. Maybe it was an expensive purchase that you *had to have* because all of your friends had it, and then you suddenly decided it wasn't necessary. Did you create a reason to keep the item, or decide to return it?

I experienced buyer's remorse early in my retail career after I made the aptly named "bad hire." Rather than admit that I had made a hiring mistake, I looked for those few good things about the person that justified the hiring decision. Of course, I was lying to myself to remove the discomfort.

Interviewer Discomfort

More important to the interview process is what I call interviewer discomfort. It is a process that takes place between you and the interviewer in the first few minutes that, if you've created a powerful first impression, almost guarantees that you will get the job you want.

Interviewer discomfort is based on how advertising works, and it differs from buyer's remorse in that one experiences mental discomfort because he or she *didn't* make the purchase that he or she believes he or she should have.

All of those late-night infomercials that say we need to be thinner or richer attempt to create mental discomfort in us that will lead to a desire to purchase the get-rich-quick product or thigh-thinner machine that will restore our feeling that we are okay. Savvy producers will also make every attempt to create a powerful first impression by using some well-respected celebrity to peddle the goods!

Ever wonder how there can be so many infomercials on in the middle of the night? It's because people such as you and me watch them and occasionally buy the products. And we just don't watch them. We sit and listen to the testimonials that say "you too can lose 10 pounds in your first week—if you just buy now."

Yes, we actually look for more reasons to buy the product to relieve the discomfort in our mind. The end result is that we either buy, or we decide not to buy and change the channel. Either way the discomfort has been removed.

Interviewer discomfort stems from the creation of a need in the mind of the interviewer that must now be dealt with through the taking of action. Every interviewer experiences some form of mental discomfort (either positive or negative) during the first few minutes of an interview, whether he or she is aware of it or not. This normally takes the form of either an instant interest in you, or an instant dislike of you. Your goal is to create a need in the mind of the interviewer that he or she must have the product *you* are selling, which is yourself!

This means that your first few minutes of your interview is *your personal infomercial*! It is imperative that you portray a powerful first impression to cause the hiring manager to "buy," and not change the channel! Once an interviewer decides in his mind that you are an applicant he would like to add to the team, he puts himself in a state of mental discomfort and continues to look for more reasons to hire you to relieve it.

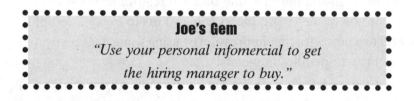

Joe's Gem
"Use your personal infomercial to get the hiring manager to buy."

Your powerful first impression turns the interviewer's mental discomfort into a persuasive power, as it practically "persuades" the interviewer to buy what you are selling—you!

Likewise, once the interviewer decides that you would not be a good candidate, the mental discomfort is such that the interviewer continues looking for more reasons to turn you down, and whatever you say after that won't really matter. This is why I no longer interview candidates longer than it is necessary to make a decision.

Once you begin looking for this effect in your daily life, you'll discover its power also applies when interacting with coworkers, fellow students, and, as a side benefit, members of the opposite sex.

Real Life

Steve was an intelligent candidate who had recently graduated from high school and was looking for a job to start earning some college cash. He created a powerful first impression and caused me to have an instant interest in him. Within a few minutes, I was already running through my mind the possibilities of what department I could place him in. I decided he would be a great fit for technology, especially since the back-to-school season would soon be upon us and we would need some help there. As we chatted, I continued to look for more reasons to hire him, and that's when the proverbial roof caved in. I learned that he was going to go to college on a scholarship (out of town to Ohio State) and that he would be leaving in late August. I nodded okay and silently did the math in my head. I would have him for 90 days—still enough time to make an impact. I then learned that he also needed two weeks off in June for a family reunion in Colorado that had already been planned. Okay, another setback, but one I could probably schedule around. Lastly, Steve added that he would probably also need a week or two off to travel to Ohio for freshman orientation as school approached. I silently sat there as I contemplated his list of demands, always remembering that the average associate only stays with the company six months anyway. I made the hire (even in the face of conflicting information) because I had already decided to do so in the first few minutes. Steve lasted around three months with me and tore it up while he was there— another satisfying hire.

Stereotypes and Discrimination

Any discussion on first impressions would not be complete if it did not cover the issue of stereotypes and discrimination. We hear quite often of someone not getting a job, home, or other opportunity because of their race, sex, age, ethnicity, economic status, or disability. I have known hiring managers who have turned down applicants because of their weight, or because they were just not very good looking.

Please don't make the mistake of confusing a first impression with discrimination. Discrimination is an inner trait of the interviewer and one that you cannot prepare for or change. It is also illegal and should not be tolerated at any cost.

If you are an applicant with a disability but can still perform the job requirements with a reasonable accommodation, you should still be considered for any available position after making the interviewer aware of that fact.

Making Interviewer Discomfort Work for You

Now that you know something about what mental discomfort an interviewer goes through during the interview, you're ready to discover exactly what you need to do to use this effect to your advantage in the interview process. So, let's discover what qualities you'll need to do this!

Chapter 3

Become an Overnight Success:

Practice Makes Perfect

The actor practices his craft day after day, waiting for his opportunity to be in front of the casting director for his few minutes so that he can become that overnight success and bask in his 15 minutes of fame.

We would all like to get the job we want in our first interview—our first attempt. However, as the actor does, we must also practice our craft in order to be ready to give our performance when called upon. There are many facets to an interview, and I will take you through the steps so that you can be at your very best in each.

Your first impression in an interview begins from the very first second of the greeting and continues through the first few minutes. What exactly happens in those first few minutes, and how is it possible for you to create such a powerful first impression that it will last through the entire interview and allow you to get the job you want?

I've broken down the typical application and interview process into two simple steps to make the process more manageable:

1. Preaudition.
2. Audition.

These two steps represent the gauntlet that you must get through to determine whether or not the interviewer is going to consider you as a legitimate candidate for the job. It is imperative that you create a positive first impression in each step in order to have your best chance of securing a job.

Fail to be on the top of your game in either step, and you're history and it's on to the next candidate. We'll cover both of them in depth in subsequent chapters, but a brief review of each follows.

Preaudition Step

The *preaudition* step is everything that takes place before you arrive at the company for your interview, with many of the decisions being made outside your presence. It is at this point in the process that certain assumptions must be made about you before you are actually interviewed.

These decisions are strictly based on instinct and sometimes have no basis in fact, other than the feeling that you would be a turndown if interviewed. The key to making a powerful first impression here is not to stand out in such a way that the gatekeepers think you are "different" or "difficult."

Some of the *preaudition* steps include:

- ◆ Applications (both paper and electronic).
- ◆ Resumes.
- ◆ Telephone etiquette.

In Hollywood, there is a joke that it is every script reader's job to give a "pass" or turndown on every screenplay he or she reads, simply for the fact that no one wants to be associated with a movie that bombs and be the one blamed for approving (or "greenlighting") the screenplay.

It sometimes gets to the point that everyone looks for reasons to turn down a screenplay rather than find a reason to get it made. (I guess this explains the sad state of Hollywood, but that's a different book.)

The same holds true in the service industry. Similar to the Hollywood reader, no one wants to greenlight someone who later turns out to be a bad hire. Also, management is pressed for time and normally cannot interview every candidate that submits an application.

Thus, most businesses have a *preaudition* process where they weed certain individuals out of consideration. This is the same screening process that headhunters normally use when looking for management or highly specialized candidates before they turn the applicant over to the hiring managers.

Audition Step

You made it through the *preaudition* step and are now set up for an interview. Now what?

The *audition* step begins from the moment you arrive for your interview. In this phase you are under scrutiny from the moment you check in to announce your arrival. I know many hiring managers who will turn down an applicant at this point without even interviewing him or her.

Most retail businesses are continually busy and there is never a good time for managers to interview, so sometimes the wait can be substantial. When I am in the middle of a customer-service issue, I might keep an applicant waiting 30 minutes or longer. Other companies, especially in the fast-food industry, only have certain hours during which they interview applicants.

Some managers like to use what's called a stress test in the industry and keep applicants waiting to see how they handle the delay. If you can't handle the stress at this point, it's a pretty good bet you are not a good service-industry candidate.

The *audition* step is actually made up four parts, three of which take place outside the realm of questioning and occur within minutes of each other upon your arrival at the company you are interviewing with. The fourth, which is the audition itself, is the actual act of interviewing (the question and answer portion):

- ◆ Body talk.
- ◆ Cute meet.
- ◆ Tangible Intangibles.
- ◆ Audition.

Each step is important in its own way, and the importance of creating a powerful first impression in each step cannot be overstated.

Body Talk

People like to hire others who are similar to themselves. If you appear unusually nervous or—heaven forbid—neurotic, you'll be out the door before you know it.

There have been studies done on nonverbal communication and how it can negatively impact an interview. This is because your body "talks" about you all of the time: the way you walk, the way you sit, your facial expressions (is it any wonder that your smile is the thing that talks best about you, and it is totally nonverbal?).

Have you ever seen a friend at school and been able to tell exactly what kind of day she was having by her body talk? The slumped shoulders, pained facial expression, and low-energy level are usually dead giveaways that things are going rather poorly. What if you saw this same person on another day with a high energy level and a beaming smile—things must be going pretty well!

The body talk step begins from the moment you arrive for the interview and continues until the interview is completed. In order to create a powerful first impression, you must eliminate any negative, self-defeating behaviors as much as possible. Oftentimes, these are the very things that we do without consciously realizing it. Some examples of negative behaviors include:

- Arriving late for the interview.
- Being rude to an associate.
- Dressing improperly.
- Becoming agitated due to having to wait for the interviewer.

- ◆ Having extremely poor nonverbal communication.
- ◆ Constantly shaking your leg or foot.
- ◆ Swiveling in your chair.
- ◆ Not looking the interviewer in the eye.
- ◆ Slouching in your seat.
- ◆ Playing with your ring, or some other object.
- ◆ Having to shut off your cell phone once the interview has started.
- ◆ Chewing gum.
- ◆ Performing funny eye or facial movements.

Cute Meet

Nearly every great screenplay (especially romantic comedies) has what producers call a "cute meet." This is when the two leads meet each other in some unusual or significant way that sets the tone for the relationship, often changing their lives forever. In *Romancing the Stone,* Jack Colton saves Joan Wilder from the villain chasing after the map she carries. In *Lethal Weapon*, Roger Murtaugh meets Martin Riggs during a takedown in the police station. Both of the scenes introduce the characters to each other in a colorful way that creates a powerful first impression and is sure to make an impact.

Although your meeting with your interviewer would hopefully be less dangerous, it still must be memorable to the point that you will be remembered for something you said or did. To create a powerful first impression, you must stand out in such a way that you become an irresistible hire, and exhibit a manner that says to the interviewer that you are someone that must be on his or her team.

Tangible Intangibles

This step is one the most important because you are now sitting face to face with your interviewer. Impress me here and you're on your way to getting greenlighted. However, I will warn you that this is also where I make the majority of my turndowns!

Think about some of the job turndowns you have had in your recent past. You passed the application test with honors— maybe you even wrote a nice little resume in a school career workshop, sounded pleasant on the telephone when the interview appointment was set, and arrived a few minutes early for the interview in your newly purchased outfit.

You made a nice, memorable comment upon greeting the interviewer and calmly sat in your seat across from him or her at the start. Yet you still left the interview without the job! What happened?

Execution Is a Must

I took my wife out for our first Valentine's date many years ago at an expensive seafood restaurant that I had always wanted to go to but couldn't afford. I saved my money and looked forward to the visit for weeks. I remember entering the restaurant and experiencing sensory overload from the delicate smells of the seafood and the visual delight of the elaborate interior decorations. The maitre d' treated us as though we were royalty. How proud I felt walking into a place such as that with my girl. It was a perfect, powerful first impression!

We both the ordered the king crab legs—our favorite— even though there was no price listed. I had never ordered anything in a restaurant at "market price," so that in itself was a little anxiety-provoking, but I made as though it was no big deal. A perfect start to a perfect evening—until the food came! The crab legs were anything but king—maybe an over-cooked little prince years away from the throne. And then there was that check...that almost made me choke.

I learned that night that all the preparation and buildup in the world is meaningless if the desired result is not achieved in the end because of lack of execution.

This may be hard for you to swallow, but you probably didn't get the job in your previous interviews because you left the interviewer wanting more—just as I wanted more at the restaurant. All your preparation went for naught because you failed to execute in the interview when necessary.

You *must* execute during the first few minutes once you are in the interview and attempting to create a powerful first impression. Your history is irrelevant until the interviewer has begun probing your past, and by then your first impression has already been made. No resume or referral is going to save you if you bomb out in the first minute. It doesn't even matter if your dad and the interviewer were fraternity brothers (unless, of course, the latter owes the former a huge favor!)

The service industry is a demanding business that relies on low-paid associates to deliver high-quality customer service. This is one of the reasons why the turnover is so high. Most companies discover that associates who are not engaged in what they do eventually burn out and seek employment elsewhere after around six months. Because most service jobs are easily trainable, intangible qualities are a must for you to have.

The Must-Have Intangibles

I am sometimes asked when I am out for lunch in my uniform, or by a customer in the store, what it takes for one to work at Circuit City. What skills does one need to be a good employee?

In the past, I would always give what I now consider lame answers. That one has to enjoy selling technology or entertainment products to customers. That they should enjoy helping solve customer issues at the customer-service counter. And that they should be detail oriented to merchandise product. Not exactly recruitment material.

But, as I thought long and hard about the question for several months, I began analyzing exactly what was it that made our store so successful for so long. What were we doing as a management team that perhaps was instinctual and not clearly defined and articulated?

If I could distill everything down into three attributes about what makes a great retail or service-industry associate, what would I look for? Would I look for great sales skills? Great customer-service skills? And what would those skills look like? How could I break them down so that they can be demonstrated in an interview so the applicant could create a powerful first impression?

After much deliberation, I defined the three intangible attributes that will give you the absolute best chance to get the job you want. These are the ones that I have identified as the best predictors of success. Give me an associate with these three intangible attributes and chances are my management team can develop them into a star:

- High-octane energy.
- Killer confidence.
- Engaging friendliness.

Now that you know what intangible qualities are needed, they must be made "tangible." By that, I mean the qualities must be identified, strengthened, and exploited to your advantage in an interview as if they were as tangible an item as the clothing you wear.

High-Octane Energy

I don't believe there is any substitute for a high energy level, or what I like to call high octane. High-octane individuals, like the premium gasoline grade, give the employer the most performance for the money. Spend several minutes in any retail business and the high-octane associates will jump out at you. They are the ones who move quickly, juggle several customers and tasks at once, and always appear to be moving on to another project while their low-octane sister associates appear to be standing still. For example:

- The waitress who expeditiously handles several customers at once without serving your steak to your neighbor in the next booth.
- The mechanic who can work on multiple cars without leaving your wheels off.
- The sales associate who can simultaneously juggle three different customers and still get quality add-on sales.
- The grocery checkout clerk who appears to be handling customers three times faster than her fellow associates on either side of her.

Any savvy employer knows that high octane equals high execution. These individuals are worth their weight in gold and can oftentimes do the work of two low-octane associates. They are also the individuals who "knock or ping" less under pressure, because they deliver top-quality work by the required deadline.

Real Life

I greeted Bob, a warehouse applicant more than a few pounds overweight who, as I walked towards him, appeared so lethargic that I thought he was going to fall asleep. He didn't even stand up to greet me, instead continuing to sit in his chair while he meekly shook my hand for what seemed to be an eternity. The deal-breaker, though, was when he used my hand to pull himself up from out of the chair, as if I were a teammate pulling my good buddy off of the ground after a great tackle. The stunt took me by surprise and almost caused me to fall down on him. This was such low octane that perhaps the tank was empty. Can you imagine motivating this guy every morning? I couldn't, and I didn't.

My top performers at Circuit City are all high-octane associates who can both multibrain and multitask, as well as handle immediate business needs. These are the individuals who are immediately identified as future departmental leads or managerial candidates.

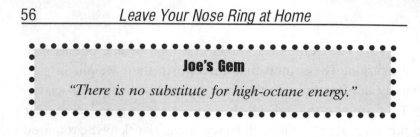

Joe's Gem

"There is no substitute for high-octane energy."

Killer Confidence

Nothing quite gives off a powerful first impression the way killer confidence does. Confidence is loosely defined as belief in one's abilities (self-confidence), although it can also mean one is confident in a situation (as in feeling certain an event or specific outcome will take place).

Jack Canfield, cocreator of the *Chicken Soup for the Soul* series, states in his book *The Success Principles* (highly recommended!) that one of the great strategies for success is to act as if you are already where you want to be. That means thinking, acting, and feeling that you have already achieved your goal.

Nothing could be closer to the truth when it comes to the job interview. If you interview as though you already have the job, chances are you will end up getting it. Service-industry applicants so rarely have killer confidence that the ones who do light up the room and silently shout, "Hire me!" The trick is in not coming across as if you are entitled to the job.

Chutzpah is the term for anyone with the shameless audacity to do whatever it takes to make it. In Hollywood, there is a story of how Steven Spielberg set up an office on the set of a movie studio before he even had a deal to be there. I have also known screenwriter wannabes who have sent their screenplays to producers and studios with gimmicks that are integral to the storyline in order to stand out from the rest of the slush pile that the Hollywood script readers read from. It's legend that *The Ticking Man* screenplay was passed around with a clock attached, which symbolized the protagonist's dilemma.

I had always attempted to discover what was unique about certain Hollywood literary agents I was interested in and then use it to my advantage to get my screenplays read. I once read in the trade paper *Daily Variety* that an agent I was interested in loved chocolate chip cookies, so I had a delivery service take over some Mrs. Fields along with a copy of the screenplay I had just finished. I'm proud to report that it did the trick! The agent loved the cookies and "greenlighted" them —however, he was less enthusiastic about the writing and "passed" on the screenplay!

Real Life

The week after Christmas is the busiest time of year for car electronics, because everyone brings in the car stereos they received as gifts to have them installed in their vehicles. I had already done my Christmas hiring for the season, but continually received calls throughout December from an applicant named Dennis, a wanna-be car-electronics installer with absolutely no experience except the usual anecdotal family and friend installations. I finally relented due to his persistence and set him up for an interview even though a trainee installer was the last thing my shop manager wanted to see during the holiday season. Even though I wasn't sold on Dennis's competencies, his killer confidence created such a powerful first impression that it got him the job. I believed because he believed. Oh yeah, he's still currently employed at Circuit City as a car electronics installer and is a monthly top performer. Way to go, Dennis!

What chutzpah are you bringing to the interview? What audacious thing have you done to get the job? Applicants with killer confidence believe they can learn any position and often have a strong desire to progress through the company. This is important when hiring is based on competencies rather than experience.

The hiring manager so desperately needs to fill the job opening that he wants to believe you and, more importantly, must believe you can do the job. As with our installer Dennis, killer confidence can sometimes be the one thing that gets the job.

Killer confidence can be such an alluring trait that many people make a living off of it by illegally running confidence games. It seems a week doesn't go by that I don't read a story about a widow or an older couple who was taken by a confidence man who enticed them to turn over their life's savings for some fictitious reason only to never to see the crook (or their money) again.

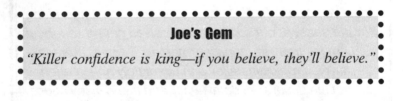

Joe's Gem

"Killer confidence is king—if you believe, they'll believe."

Engaging Friendliness

How many times have you visited a retail establishment and been waited on by someone who looked as if he or she really didn't want to be there? I'm sure you'll agree that it probably happens more often than not, because, sadly, this is the rule rather than the exception.

One of the more frequent customer complaints I hear about retail establishments is that the associates are just plain rude and don't care about the customer. Part of my success as a manager is that I have been extremely fortunate to hire associates with engaging friendliness, which reflects in my monthly customer-service survey scores and add-on sales.

Engaging friendliness is more than just having a nice smile and an outgoing disposition. Outgoing associates sell well—engaged, friendly associates sell *big*! It's having a charming, winning personality that disarms customers in such a way that they lose any "salesperson resistance." Engaged, friendly associates involve themselves with their customer and take an active role in their satisfaction.

Real Life

Although my primary job as Store Director while on the sales floor is to ensure that all customers are being helped and are having a great experience they would tell their friends about, I always attempt to thank the customers who have made a purchase before they leave the store. It's sort of a mini exit interview to see that all their needs were satisfied. I noticed Elaine, a customer in the imaging department, gathering a few bags loaded with a digital camera, photo printer, accessories, and our Circuit City Advantage-Protection Plan. Realizing that she made a rather large purchase, I made it a point to go over and thank her for shopping with us and not one of our competitors. Elaine quickly blurted out how well Josie, our product specialist loaded with engaging friendliness, took extremely good care of her and got her everything she needed. She jokingly added that she only came into the store to purchase a camera that was in our ad for $200, but ended up spending nearly $1,100 because Josie had gotten her everything she needed, which she greatly appreciated. What a great compliment about a part-time associate (who's also a full-time mom) who only works because she genuinely wants to help others. Josie rocks!

Applicants with engaging friendliness create a powerful first impression and are gems to any hiring manager that deals with the public. One can immediately envision them on a sales floor identifying and satisfying customer needs, or at a customer-service counter empathizing with a customer over a problem they are having. Food servers with this attribute are money in the bank because they are excellent with add-on sales due to the strong rapport they build with their guests.

Sales associates with engaging friendliness have a knack for insinuating themselves into the customer's space so that they seldom get the dreaded "just looking" reply when they approach a customer. Customer-service associates with this trait are especially adept at calming irate customers down because they have an innate skill at displaying empathy in a way that makes the customer feels that they are truly being heard.

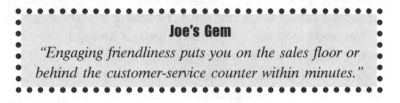

Joe's Gem

"Engaging friendliness puts you on the sales floor or behind the customer-service counter within minutes."

Rosa, the associate of mine I mentioned in a previous chapter, had an engaging friendliness that just put one at ease when communicating. It was the reason we talked for nearly 30 minutes even though I knew within minutes that she would be hired!

Engaging friendliness is not seen only in the business arena. Have you ever gone to a friend's house where you simply felt "at home" and then gone to another's house where you felt as if you were a stranger?

My wife has a friend, Jackie, who could be called the perfect hostess. When I'm over at Jackie's house, I never have to worry about feeling like a stranger. Even though she's a busy mom, she still has time to check on me to see if I need anything to eat or drink, ask me if there's a football game that I want to watch, and provide me with the day's paper. A prime example of engaged friendliness every time I'm over!

Another great example is a television show that continues to generate the ratings. While taking a break from writing this book, I spent a few moments with my family, who was watching the latest installment of the *American Idol* auditions, and I noticed a peculiar thing. A female singer entered the audition room with such a powerful first impression (the high-octane energy, the killer confidence, and the engaging friendliness) that the judges remarked about it in their opening chat with her.

She didn't sound all that good doing her Whitney Houston impression—not terrible, but just not on a par with some of the other singers. However, she had created such a powerful first impression in those first few minutes that the judges said how sweet she was and how much they liked her and that, even though it wasn't the best singing they had heard, she deserved to go to Hollywood because she had what they were looking for in the next American Idol. How's that for engaging friendliness!

Audition

Mention the word *audition* to anyone and it possibly conjures up a vision of an actor or actress having just a few minutes to get into a character and give his or her best performance to get a coveted role or part in a production.

This is what you must do at your audition (your interview), only the character is one you should know how to play very well. You!

This being the last step in the application process, it's great news if you've gotten this far. The bad news is that this is where applicants sometimes freeze up, forget their "lines," and fail to continue their powerful first impression. This is the moment you have been working towards, when you are on the stage in front of your hiring manager, and the most critical time in needing an award-winning performance to get the job you want.

You've demonstrated high-octane energy, held the interviewer's interest with your killer confidence, and built rapport by being engagingly friendly. Now the panic begins to set in as the interviewer starts to focus on those dreaded questions! You know which ones—the 150 you were supposed to have memorized the night before!

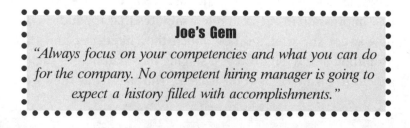

Joe's Gem

"Always focus on your competencies and what you can do for the company. No competent hiring manager is going to expect a history filled with accomplishments."

The thing you must remember is that you have already demonstrated the intangibles needed by almost every service-industry employer. The hiring manager wants you and needs you! You have already learned that at this point in the interview he or she is merely validating his reaction to your powerful first impression and is looking for more reasons to hire you.

Upgrade Your Mind's Processor

You're probably now wondering how to get the intangible qualities of high-octane energy, killer confidence, and engaging friendliness if you don't have them. That's a logical question!

Wouldn't it be cool if we could give ourselves a "processor upgrade," similar to what happens in the technology world? What if I said you *could* upgrade your mind similar to the way one upgrades his or her computer? What if you could eliminate the "signal degradation" in your mind and express your thought processes with perfect clarity the way the new digital televisions do?

All of the above *is* possible. You just have to want it. My job will be to give you the "instruction manual" and take you through it step-by-step. Your job will be to integrate yourself into the process and complete the required steps. Yes, I know it would be more convenient to pay an assembly fee and just have someone else do the upgrade for you, but unfortunately we'll have to leave that to future generations!

Let's get digital!

Chapter 4

Get Digital:

Programming Yourself for Success

The actor continually envisions himself in the role until the character is so clear he could play the part in his sleep. Then, once on the stage with the lights shining and the audience watching, his trembling fear again shows its ugly face and prevents him from portraying the one character he has known so well.

A bad self-image is similar to bad credit: It's only going to get worse unless one stops the negative behavior and begins repairing it today. If you are not creating a powerful first impression, it's possible that you are sabotaging your chance before you even walk into the room to greet the interviewer.

There are many great self-help books available for one to improve one's self-esteem, and certainly the topic is beyond the scope of this book. However, I don't believe one can completely cover the topic of creating a powerful first impression without briefly covering the issue of self-image and the impact it has on the interviewing process.

Digital Revolution

The world has experienced a digital revolution that has changed the way we live. Digital sound and video have transformed our telephones, recordings, and televisions. Digital technology allows one to create a recording with very high fidelity, and then give a perfect reproduction every time (as there is little or no signal degradation), in a way that analog never could.

A great way to visualize the difference between digital and analog is to think of two radios—one with a digital tuner dial that has distinct station numbers, such as 102.7, and another with an analog tuner dial that has the old wheel that must be rotated to tune a station in.

When you lock in a digitally tuned station, the signal never leaves that frequency. It is clear and precise. What happens when you tune in a station on an analog radio? Have you ever experienced a station going in and out? A station filled with static? A station that drifts from one radio channel to another so often that it is difficult to focus in on the one you want? And what happens when you drive under a railroad viaduct? More radio drift.

This is the way your mind reacts, only instead of poor frequency and static, you experience confusion, fear, anxiety, and doubt.

Have you joined the digital revolution, or are the analog audio and video tapes still playing in your head? Do most people see you as a winner or as a whiner?

Are the negative, audio recordings so pervasive that you now hear yourself saying how you'll never be a winner during your waking day? Is your life filled with such signal degradation that you sometimes live with confusion, fear, anxiety, and doubt?

Join the Revolution

I'm always amused when applicants are prepped to answer the question "where do you see yourself in five years?" The sad truth is that many applicants don't even know where they see themselves tomorrow. They sometimes live in a world that bounces them from crisis to crisis, hoping to land somewhere at the end near their fantasy at the end, but most times it does not happen.

Isn't it about time for you to revolt against your analog mind and exchange it for a digitalized version that knows exactly what it wants both today *and* five years into the future?

Fuzzy Picture

Do you often get a fuzzy picture when you look at your analog video tapes? No, I don't mean the ones you put in your old VCR—I mean the ones playing in your head. You know the ones I mean. The tape of you going into your job interview, making a powerful first impression, answering every question perfectly, and then the hiring manager standing up to shake your hand to welcome you to the team—the one that never happens. The tape with such poor quality that the images cannot be transferred to your real life with digital quality, because of the fear you experience in the hiring manager's office.

Maybe you fantasize about a certain someone who is the love of your dreams—you see yourself on a picnic with him or her, sitting under a large oak tree with a breeze rustling the leaves, the waves of the pond sparkling in the background. And that kiss. Yes, that kiss always happens (though maybe not in reality). That analog tape has been played so often, it's now as old and torn as the fantasy that never took place because your fear of rejection was so powerful, it prevented you from ever voicing your affection.

Yes, Freddy Krueger, the old villain from the 1980s horror flicks, is back in town torturing us once again. Only this time he's not in our dreams—he's in our reality.

You may have known for some time about using the power of visualization. You lie in your bed every night reviewing the events of the day (what you could have done, what you should have done, and what you'll do next time), but then you play the same tape the next day. Why don't those new visuals you dream ever seem to play out in your real life the way the psychologists said they would?

From the time you could walk you have heard that dreams can come true. They can—*but only if you make them happen*! Robert G. Allen, coauthor of *The One Minute Millionaire*, claims that the future you envision is the future you get. I don't believe Robert is talking about any fantasy or daydream, but about the real need for a clear, precise plan for you to achieve *beyond* your wildest dreams, and the massive action needed to execute it.

Real Life

Years ago (during those brief minutes just before I would fall asleep), I would always lie awake in my bed thinking, daydreaming really, of being at the Academy Awards. It was like I was flying above the people watching myself (psychologists call this grandstanding) sitting in the audience next to my wife. The vision would always start just as the presenters were going to announce the recipient of the Best Original Screenplay, and I would listen to them announce the nominees just as I had for many years as a young boy watching on television. I don't remember ever hearing anyone's name but my own. Then would come the seven most beautiful words I could ever hear: "and the Oscar goes to...Joe Swinger." I would make the walk to get the statue as the audience cheered and, once on stage, thank my wife for believing in me for all those years. I would then fall asleep and let my subconscious take over as I was always taught to do. Unfortunately, after many years, I never did hear those words, and I never did make that walk for the statue. It soon became time to leave the Hollywood Dream Factory and begin to take action on making my new dream (that of starting a family and becoming a published author) a reality. Now, there is still no cheering audience and no statue to receive, but I would still like to thank my wife and sons for believing in me for all those years.

Take Responsibility

What was the reason why I never became a produced screenwriter? Why was I never able to convert what I clearly envisioned thousands of times in my head into my real life? Was I just not good enough? Or was my thinking distorted (similar to the analog radio signal) because I was never able to transfer the analog vision in my head to my digital reality because *I* failed to make it happen, and because I relied upon others to do it for me?

The first step to getting digital is the most important—you *must* take responsibility for your life. It does not matter if you're 16 or 60. If you cannot accept the thought that **you** are in charge of your own destiny, please put this book back on the shelf and let someone else read it. Perhaps you'll pick it up again someday.

It seems to be the latest fad in this country that one is entitled to everything one wants. We want lower taxes, but demand government assistance in many areas. We want the lowest prices, but expect the absolute best customer service. We crave the best education, but feel entitled to student loans we don't plan on paying back. We expect the best paying jobs, but don't want to pay our dues. Even love has become an entitlement, because some of us are so wrapped up in ourselves that we don't feel the need to reciprocate.

Take responsibility for your life—right this second—and proclaim your freedom from a confused analog mind. If you haven't already begun, scream loud and clear: "I'm going digital!"

Attributes

Digital and analog minds have different attributes and these result in clarity (digital) or degradation (analog). We've already covered some previously, but here's a review with a few additional ones:

Digital Mind	Analog Mind
Energetic	Lethargic
Confident	Anxious
Risk-taking	Fearful
Enthusiastic	Apprehensive
Determined	Doubtful
Inspired	Confused
Accepting	Judgmental
Empowered	Impotent
Charitable	Envious

Where do you see yourself? It is not uncommon to have attributes from both types (some analog and some digital), and you may even waver between the two states depending on the stress in your life at the present moment.

Know Your PFI Index

We talked in a previous chapter about the necessity of having the three tangible intangibles of high-octane energy, killer confidence, and engaging friendliness to create a powerful first impression. I call the combination of these three intangibles one's Positive First Impression Index (PFI Index).

To help you find your PFI Index, we need to convert the intangibles to a number that is measurable and can be made useful. In order to get this number, I've created an un-scientific survey for you to estimate how you currently see yourself.

Obtaining Your PFI Index

To obtain the index, you will get an individual score for each of the three intangibles that you'll want to demonstrate in the interview. When you add your three numbers together, you'll have your total score.

Now, as do a lot of us, you might inflate your score and rate yourself higher than what others might score. However, the index is still a good indication of where you probably rate on the three items, and how powerful your first impression might be.

Because the index estimates what you think about yourself, and others may see you differently, it would be a good idea to have another person also rate you and then you can average the results. The difference in scores may surprise you!

Read the following and then choose the response that best fits you. Your state of mind can change frequently, but try to rate yourself as you think you would normally perform over a longer period of time. This an open book-test, and no one but you will see the score, so be honest!

High-Octane Energy

1—Strongly Agree	4—Disagree
2—Agree	5—Strongly Disagree
3—Sometimes	

1.   I like being alone. ___
2.   I don't like to make immediate or long-range goals. ___
3.   I usually don't get much done during the day. ___

4.   I feel like I am just existing. ___

5.   I only do what's necessary in my life,
     in school, and on my job. ___

6.   I'm often tired. ___

7.   I often have trouble getting out of bed in the morning
     to start my day. ___

8.   I don't like challenges and often feel overwhelmed. ___

9.   I procrastinate because I can't gather
     the energy to get started. ___

10. It's difficult for me to get excited
     or enthusiastic about anything. ___

Add your **High-Octane Energy** *points*: _____

If your total is:

45–50! give yourself a High-Octane Energy *score* of 5

35–44! give yourself a High-Octane Energy *score* of 4

25–34! give yourself a High-Octane Energy *score* of 3

15–24! give yourself a High-Octane Energy *score* of 2

10–14! give yourself a High-Octane Energy *score* of 1

High-Octane Energy *score*: _____

Killer Confidence

1—Strongly Agree   4—Disagree

2—Agree   5—Strongly Disagree

3—Sometimes

1.   I feel I am unattractive. ___

2.   I am not as smart as others. ___

3.   I tend to make mistakes. ___

4.   I wish I was someone else. ___

5.   I worry that I will appear foolish to others. ___

6.   I'm afraid to try anything new or different. ___

7.   I fear failure. ___

8.   My rewards in life are generally outside my control. ___

9.   I can't seem to fit in. ___

10. There is nothing I'm really good at. ___

Add your **Killer Confidence** *points*: _____

If your total is:

45–50! give yourself a Killer Confidence *score* of 5

35–44! give yourself a Killer Confidence *score* of 4

25–34! give yourself a Killer Confidence *score* of 3

15–24! give yourself a Killer Confidence *score* of 2

10–14! give yourself a Killer Confidence *score* of 1

Killer Confidence *score*: _____

Engaging Friendliness

1—Strongly Agree   4—Disagree

2—Agree   5—Strongly Disagree

3—Sometimes

1.   I am not an active listener. ___

2.   I like to keep to myself. ___

3.   Most people don't have anything of value
     or interest to say. ___

4.   I tend to be judgmental. ___

5.   I don't like to make eye contact. ___

6.   I don't particularly care what others think or feel. ___

7.   I enjoy proving others wrong. ___

8.   I would rather talk about myself than hear about others. ___

9.   I don't enjoy talking with new people. ___

10. I don't make friends easily. ___

Add your **Engaging Friendliness** *points*: _____

If your total is:

45–50! give yourself an Engaging Friendliness *score* of 5

35–44! give yourself an Engaging Friendliness *score* of 4

25–34! give yourself an Engaging Friendliness *score* of 3

15–24! give yourself an Engaging Friendliness *score* of 2

10–14! give yourself an Engaging Friendliness *score* of 1

Engaging Friendliness *score*: _____

Your PFI Index

Your PFI Index should give you a fairly good estimate of how you might compare to others in the eyes of your interviewer. This also now gives us a common language when speaking about the intangibles.

Tally your three scores from the previous pages:

High-Octane Energy score   _____

Killer Confidence score   +_____

Engaging Friendliness score   +_____

PFI Index   =_____

+ Score of 13–15: Extremely high powerful first impression index. You should be able to go into any service-industry business and get the job within a few minutes. You are the total package that seldom seems to walk through the door.

+ Score of 10–12: Good powerful first impression index. You are still a great candidate to get the job in the first few minutes. You are also a person who can be developed into a winning associate if put into a position that utilizes your strengths.

- Score of 6–9: Average powerful first impression index. You may be the average applicant that walks through the door on a regular basis.
- Score of 3–5: Below-average powerful first impression index. You may need several interviews before getting a service-industry job.

Now that you have your PFI Index and can see where you rank, do you think that you are creating a powerful first impression in your interviews or is something missing that is preventing you from having the desired effect?

Your PFI Index in the Real World

Your PFI Index should be a good estimate as to whether you are creating a powerful first impression during your job interviews and, if not, whether you might need to exhibit more energy, confidence, friendliness, or some combination of each in future interviews.

This can also be a very effective tool for you to use when hiring managers have several openings and you are undecided about what department to interview for. I sometimes interview good applicants who are not quite sure what department they want to work in, so I'll often ask them what area of the business (music and movies, MP3, and so on) they see themselves enjoying and being most successful in.

The applicant's response is usually pretty close to what I would estimate their PFI Index to look like. An example would be a male applicant low in engaging friendliness who says that he could see himself working in the warehouse. Chances are this person prefers working in an environment that has little interaction with the customers.

Thus, if you rated yourself as having high confidence and high friendliness, you might do well as a sales associate. Or, if you were rated with high energy and high friendliness, you might make a great customer-service associate.

The index can also be useful for you to recruit other associates for your company. Anytime you go to a restaurant or mall and interact with other employees, it is a good time to notice if any of them would make a great associate like yourself and also be fun to work with. It would take seconds to quickly estimate in your head what a person's PFI Index would be. This is good practice.

Even though my associates have no idea about the PFI Index, they often tell me about someone they met while out to lunch who they thought would make a great employee. When I ask them why, it is always because the employee made a powerful first impression on my associate.

My wife will sometimes come home from shopping and tell me that she was helped by a "14" and that I should go recruit her. Is it scientifically valid? No, but the fact that what my wife says is based on the sales associate's powerful first impression makes the rating very effective, relevant, and usable.

Now that we've seen how the PFI Index works in the real world, let's discover how you can go about increasing your score by identifying how you view your interaction in *your* world.

Motivation

We have not yet discussed one very important factor in a powerful first impression: How motivated are you for success? This is one of those questions where everyone believes they are highly motivated—we all want success—but upon deeper introspection discovers that they may not be.

Are you motivated enough to risk failure in front of your family and friends? Are you motivated enough to shout your goals to the world and then *have* to succeed or have the world know that you have failed?

How much control do you feel you have over your life? Are you living *your* life or someone else's? Do you feel that where you are at this point in your life is the result of *your* decisions, or your parents, friends, and culture?

It is extremely difficult for you to demonstrate the necessary qualities of a powerful first impression if you feel you have no control over your life. Why would you feel as though you had control in the interview when you can control little else?

I said at the beginning of this chapter that you must take responsibility for your life this very second. What if I said it is easier for you to get control over your life than you think? What if you could uncork the high-octane energy and engaging friendliness within you that is just waiting to be tapped as if a rich oil well?

I wrote in a previous chapter that killer confidence is king, and I meant that. If you take away one concept from this chapter, it is this: Killer confidence, once ignited, automatically becomes a fuel for high-octane energy and engaging friendliness.

Killer confidence is the fuel that will burst through the analog mind traits of doubt, anxiety, and fear. High-octane energy and engaging friendliness automatically increase because your energy is no longer being dissipated by negative thoughts.

What if I could show you how to increase your self-confidence and, as a by-product, increase your high-octane energy and engaging friendliness?

Joe's Gem

"Killer confidence, once ignited, automatically becomes a fuel for your high-octane energy and engaging friendliness."

Your Big Yellow School Bus

Locus of Control (LOC), developed by Julian Rotter in 1966, measures how much control you believe you have over your life, and whether or not the rewards you receive are of your own doing. Although it's good to know the psychological term, you can think of it as your own big, yellow school bus parked outside of your house every morning ready for you to go to that day's lesson on life.

Close your eyes and visualize the bus clearly in your mind. Can you see your name written on the side of it? Picture yourself coming out of your house in the morning and walking towards the street to get on the bus. Maybe there are even a few friends and family members milling around waiting for you to get on. Now, grab a seat and get ready to experience today's lesson.

Do you sometimes feel as if life is filled with weekly emergencies of some sort? Does your life sometimes seem to be going in a different direction than you would like it to, as if your bus has turned left but you wanted to go right? Do you act, or react, to events in your life?

What seat position did you get in when you boarded your bus? Was it the driver's seat or a seat at the rear? Who was driving? Do you feel that this person drives your life?

Were you ready and willing to fight the traffic and poor drivers on the road of life and drive the bus to where you wanted to go—and experience your life on your terms—or did you prefer to go into the back of the bus (where it is safer) and relax with a book or friends while others drove you around? Maybe you were even content to stare out the window in a daydream state and just watch life pass you by.

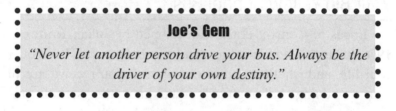

Joe's Gem

"Never let another person drive your bus. Always be the driver of your own destiny."

It is a must for you to know your own LOC. You cannot have true killer confidence if you are a passenger on a bus being driven by someone else. You can only control your own destiny if *you are the driver of your own bus!*

See who's driving your bus this instant! Take the following Rotter Locus of Control Questionnaire and see what your score is.

Rotter's Locus of Control Scale

Choose the one statement from each pair with which you agree. You may not support either statement completely, because each statement represents two extreme, opposing positions. Please choose the one you agree with more.

1. a) Children get into trouble because their parents punish them too much.

    b) The trouble with most children nowadays is that their parents are too easy with them.

2. a) Many of the unhappy things in people's lives are partly due to bad luck.

    b) People's misfortunes result from the mistakes they make.

3. a) One of the major reasons why we have wars is because people don't take enough interest in politics.

    b) There will always be wars, no matter how hard people try to prevent them.

4. a) In the long run people get the respect they deserve in this world.

    b) Unfortunately, an individual's worth often passes unrecognized no matter how hard he or she tries.

5. a) The idea that teachers are unfair to students is nonsense.

    b) Most students don't realize the extent to which their grades are influenced by accidental happenings.

6. a) Without the right breaks one cannot be an effective leader.

    b) Capable people who fail to become leaders have not taken advantage of their opportunities.

7.   a) No matter how hard you try some people just don't like you.

b) People who can't get others to like them don't understand how to get along with others.

8.   a) Heredity plays the major role in determining one's personality.

b) It is one's experiences in life which determine what they're like.

9.   a) I have often found that what is going to happen will happen.

b) Trusting to fate has never turned out as well for me as making a decision to take a definite course of action.

10. a) In the case of the well-prepared student there is rarely if ever such a thing as an unfair test.

b) Many times exam questions tend to be so unrelated to course work that studying is really useless.

11. a) Becoming a success is a matter of hard work, luck has little or nothing to do with it.

b) Getting a good job depends mainly on being in the right place at the right time.

12. a) The average citizen can have an influence in government decisions.

b) This world is run by the few people in power, and there is not much the little guy can do about it.

13. a) When I make plans, I am almost certain that I can make them work.

b) It is not always wise to plan too far ahead because many things turn out to be a matter of good or bad fortune anyhow.

14. a) There are certain people who are just no good.

b) There is some good in everybody.

15. a) In my case getting what I want has little or nothing to do with luck.

b) Many times we might just as well decide what to do by flipping a coin.

16. a) Who gets to be the boss often depends on who was lucky enough to be in the right place first.

b) Getting people to do the right thing depends upon ability; luck has little or nothing to do with it.

17. a) As far as world affairs are concerned, most of us are the victims of forces we can neither understand nor control.

b) By taking an active part in political and social affairs the people can control world events.

18. a) Most people don't realize the extent to which their lives are controlled by accidental happenings.

b) There really is no such thing as "luck."

19. a) One should always be willing to admit mistakes.

b) It is usually best to cover up one's mistakes.

20. a) It is hard to know whether or not a person really likes you.

   b) How many friends you have depends upon how nice a person you are.

21. a) In the long run the bad things that happen to us are balanced by the good ones.

   b) Most misfortunes are the result of lack of ability, ignorance, laziness, or all three.

22. a) With enough effort we can wipe out political corruption.

   b) It is difficult for people to have much control over the things politicians do in office.

23. a) Sometimes I can't understand how teachers arrive at the grades they give.

   b) There is a direct connection between how hard I study and grades I get.

24. a) A good leader expects people to decide for themselves what they should do.

   b) A good leader makes it clear to everybody what their jobs are.

25. a) Many times I feel that I have little influence over the things that happen to me.

   b) It is impossible for me to believe that chance or luck plays an important role in my life.

26. a) People are lonely because they don't try to be friendly.

b) There's not much use in trying too hard to please people; if they like you, they like you.

27. a) There is too much emphasis on athletics in high school.

b) Team sports are an excellent way to build character.

28. a) What happens to me is my own doing.

b) Sometimes I feel that I don't have enough control over the direction my life is taking.

29. a) Most of the time I can't understand why politicians behave the way they do.

b) In the long run the people are responsible for bad government on a national as well as on a local level.

Score one point for each of the following responses:

2. a	11. b	21. a
3. b	12. b	22. b
4. b	13. b	23. a
5. b	15. b	25. a
6. a	16. a	26. b
7. a	17. a	28. b
9. a	18. a	29. a
10. b	20. a	

Possible scores range from zero, as the lowest, to 23, as the highest. Your score will give you an idea of where you fall on the Locus of Control scale. There are no fixed dividing lines between high, medium, and low scores.

- A high score = External Locus of Control
- A low score = Internal Locus of Control

If you have an internal Locus of Control (low score of approximately 0–7), you believe that it is your own actions that determine your successes and failures. You are an individual who attempts to influence people and who solicits information and knowledge to ensure success from you own efforts.

If you have an external Locus of Control (high score of approximately 16–23), you believe that your own behavior doesn't matter much, and that the successes and failures in your life are outside your control. You have a greater belief that fate or destiny plays a large role in who you are and who you will become in the future.

If you are somewhere in the middle on the Locus of Control (middle score of approximately 8–15), you may take on the characteristics of both internal and external at different times of your life.

Your Locus of Control

What did your score show? Did it show that you feel that you are in charge of your own destiny, or do you make life decisions based on the needs and desires of others? What do you think your chances are for achieving your future goals based on your score? What changes do you think you will have to make in your life to create a powerful first impression and get the job you want?

Studies have identified that if you feel that you are driving your own bus, you will achieve more in school, act more independently, and feel less depressed than those who feel they are not in the driver's seat. Some studies have clearly demonstrated if you are a highly internal LOC individual, you are very determined and motivated, are a risk-taker, and, because you are more willing to wait for success, are more committed to achieving your goals.

There appears to be no question that killer confidence is a byproduct of a strong internal Locus of Control.

Observe and analyze your behavior for the next several days while going about your daily living. What do you see? Examine your rewards, accomplishments, and setbacks for the week. Did you feel they were the result of your own execution and initiative (or lack of), or were they a result of a lucky occurrence?

Joe's Gem

"Killer confidence is a by-product of a strong internal locus of control."

- ◆ Did you prepare and execute well on a school exam, or did you get a good grade because the "class curve" was in your favor?
- ◆ Did you have an awesome sales day on the job because of your confident execution, or just because the "right customer" walked in the door?

♦ Did you have a terrible sales day on the job because you arrived at work tired and in a "bad mood," or because no customers were buying that day?

♦ Did you meet an exciting member of the opposite sex because you had the confidence to walk up and engage in a conversation with her or him, or because she or he just happened to be there talking to a mutual friend of yours.

How did you feel after your observations? Did you see yourself driving your own bus or as someone who was sitting in the back being taken for a ride? Do you agree? What changes will you make in the future?

Have you discovered it is now easier to observe and listen to other people on the job or at school and determine if they are driving their own bus? It should be easy to tell—just listen to how many excuses they make for their failures and how much credit they take for their successes.

Real Life

I am responsible for "setting the pace" on the sales floor and keeping all the product specialists pumped up to maximize both sales and customer service. I often do this by speaking to each one after a customer has made a purchase, which allows me to offer praise to the associate for making the sale. I spoke with two associates in about 10 minutes regarding their customer interactions. William had a great TV sale with add-ons and stated, "I recommended everything the customer was going to need, showed them the benefits, and they bought it all like I knew they would." Veronica sold a huge computer package with accessories and software installation and stated "I couldn't believe how easy it was. I didn't have to do anything. She just kept picking out accessories and putting them into the basket." Can you determine by their comments who is driving their own bus and who is not?

I am responsible to inspire and motivate my associates so that they achieve the results that my company desires. Oftentimes, there are several simultaneous initiatives that the team is being measured on and is expected to obtain. It is imperative for me to know my people well enough to maximize their potential as an associate. I do this by knowing who in the store is driving his or her own bus and who is not.

Fear

Fear can be the most debilitating analog trait of all, and it certainly can be one of the biggest drainers on a positive first impression. Perhaps you normally experience nervousness before or during your job interview. A little anxiety is good. This is called performance anxiety, and even the best athletes experience this type of anxiety.

What separates the great ones from the mediocre is flawless execution despite it. Some studies have even shown that anxiety over an event can actually increase performance.

Fear will destroy your powerful first impression and the chance to get the job quicker than lack of preparation for the interview will. Fear makes you look weak—it makes you look desperate.

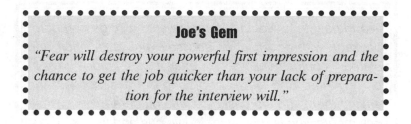

Joe's Gem

"Fear will destroy your powerful first impression and the chance to get the job quicker than your lack of preparation for the interview will."

Fear is a breeding ground for another trait that will simply destroy your dreams: procrastination. People procrastinate because they fear failure. Maybe you procrastinate on applying to college because you fear you will be rejected. Perhaps you put off beginning a creative project because you fear that you aren't good enough. Perhaps you miss application deadlines for extracurricular school activities because you fear you are not socially desirable.

Fear is the one trait that is so strong it can stop your dreams in their tracks even if you have a strong internal Locus of Control and are the driver of your own bus. Fear can cause such paralysis that even the best of us will make excuses about not having enough time, money, and luck to achieve our dreams. You must be willing to do what is necessary to overcome your fear.

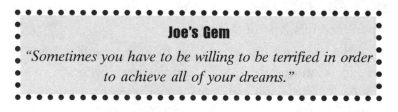

Joe's Gem

"Sometimes you have to be willing to be terrified in order to achieve all of your dreams."

John R. Noe states in his book, *Peak Performance Principles for High Achievers,* that he was a fat and flabby, out-of-shape businessman who was on the path to having a heart bypass, just as his father did, due to his sedentary lifestyle. John made a decision—that day—to get both his mind and body into shape. He began his journey by barely jogging around the block, and completed it by climbing the Matterhorn, the classic climber's mountain in Switzerland. How did he do it?

John says that fear is not something that one conquers by saying little clichés to oneself. Fear is overcome by taking action on the first step towards the immediate goal.

Use your killer confidence to lower the hammer on fear whenever it begins to show its ugly face, and take that first step right now. Identify some fears that you feel have been keeping you from achieving your goals and what you can do to eliminate them with your digital mind.

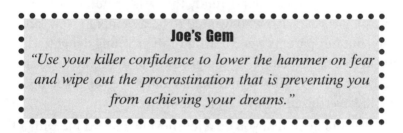

Joe's Gem

"Use your killer confidence to lower the hammer on fear and wipe out the procrastination that is preventing you from achieving your dreams."

Crayola Moments

There are moments in your life—you must look closely to recognize them—when you have an opportunity to do something extraordinary, an opportunity to affect your life so it will never be the same again, when you are presented with a situation where you must quickly decide whether to act on it or not. I call these "Crayola moments" because of the way they color our life.

Crayola moments differ from regular moments because of the effect they have on your life, although sometimes the result is not seen for years. John Noe had a Crayola moment when he decided to get into shape to avoid his bypass and climb the Matterhorn. An Olympian who wins the gold medal most likely had his or her Crayola moment four years before the victory.

Perhaps you have already experienced some yourself. A decision to get married or attend a certain school. Perhaps you changed your major in college for a reason that is not clear at the moment. Maybe the job you want was decided upon after a Crayola moment.

I sometimes think about a friend I once had who did not take advantage of an opportunity that was presented to her. I knew a girl years ago who wanted to be a model in New York City, but her parents were fearful of their young daughter living in the big city alone, so the girl gave in under the pressure and didn't move. How would her life have been changed if she could have seized that Crayola moment?

I recommend that you do a journeyline of your life with all the major turning points—your birth, schools you went to, important relationships, and so on. Do it right now on any old piece of paper! It is amazing when you see your life in journey-line form to recognize how one decision affects the next and the next one after that.

I made the comment earlier that most applicants do not know where they will be tomorrow, let alone in five years. How do you plan on answering the question "where do you see yourself in five years?" when asked in an interview? What do you want your journeyline to look like in the next five years?

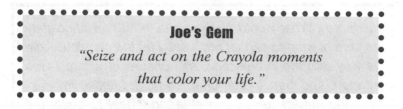

Joe's Gem

"Seize and act on the Crayola moments
that color your life."

Make today—this moment—a Crayola moment and draw your journey-line for the next five years. Put in all your goals (school, relationship, career success, and so on). Do not worry for an instant on how you will make it happen. What do you envision? Because the future you envision is the future you will get.

Real Life

I left my home in Chicago in my early 20s because I deeply felt I needed to leave in order to find my identity. As I drove west to Los Angeles, I remember pulling off at a small town somewhere in the middle of the journey, crying and trembling with fear. I tried to eat the lunch my girlfriend, who I had just said good-bye to, had made for me, but my hands were shaking too badly. I sat there questioning what I was doing—whether I was crazy or not—and then drove the car to get back on the main highway. I sat at the stop sign for what seemed like an eternity, but was probably only a moment, and quickly ran the options through my mind as if I was feeding data into a computer. What would my life be like if I turned and went back east, back towards my home? Would I be a failure? Would I ever amount to anything? At least I might know what to expect. What would my life be if I continued west, towards the unknown? What if I were to *fail there? What would everyone think? I had absolutely no idea of what to expect out west. I let the car slowly idle its way into the intersection, still unsure of where I was headed. And then, in that brief moment, I chose my destiny and quickly turned the steering wheel to guide the car west to confront my fears.*

You have done quite a bit of work on yourself throughout this chapter, and you should congratulate yourself! You've identified your PFI Index and Locus of Control. You've confronted your fears, and have taken steps to begin eliminating them.

You've learned how to identify and seize the Crayola moments in your life. You drew your journeyline and have now recognized that where you are now is the result of the decisions you have made. And you also identified where you are going to be in the next five years.

You have now experienced all of the above—plus you're loaded with high-octane energy, killer confidence, and engaging friendliness. Now, let's go show you how and where to get a job with your digital mind and powerful first impression!

Chapter 5

Market Madness:

Thinking Outside the Box

The actor goes from audition to audition, continually getting turned down for any role outside his typecast part of the punk thug. He yearns for more—knows he can play the romantic lead—but no matter how hard he tries to convince the casting directors, still no one believes or gives him the chance.

Let's say that you've had it with the service industry and decide to borrow some money from your parents and go into business for yourself. When trying to decide on a product, you think back to a drink your grandmother would always make for you on hot summer mornings when you were a kid.

It had a great taste with a mixture of fresh lemons and limes that you think would be a great seller in today's market and be worthy competition to Coke's Sprite and Pepsi's Sierra Mist.

No matter how great your product was and how much money you spent, what do you think the chances of your success would be?

Barriers to Entry

Business management uses barriers to entry to determine the difficulties encountered in entering a new industry. Whenever a company contemplates entering a new market that it is not currently in, it analyzes what are the costs involved to break in and turn a profit. The greater the barriers, the higher the cost involved.

A new soft-drink maker, such as yourself, would have to contend with the strong consumer loyalties to the brands of Coke and Pepsi in order to enter the lemon-lime market. Naturally, there would be huge difficulties to differentiate your drink from your competitors', especially from a marketing awareness point of view.

Sometimes a small market share is enough for a small company. In today's entrepreneurial society, there are many small businesses operating around the world. I know of a few moms here locally who make money selling cookies and bread they make in their homes. The Internet is another example of an industry with easy entry.

See Yourself as a Small Business

The job market, as does the soft drink industry, has its own difficulties to entry. If you think of yourself and your job skills as a product, you also have to market yourself against the "name brands," who, of course, are your competitors for the position you desire.

One of the great things about the service industry is the easy entry. I previously mentioned that turnover is extremely high and there is a continual need for talented associates who can excel at what they do. Now is the best time for you to think outside of the box and, rather than do the job that you have always done, search for the job you want by focusing on your competencies to fulfill the job's requirements.

If you see yourself as a small business, then you must do what small businesses do when they roll out a new product or service and take the steps to define yourself:

- Define your core competencies.
- Define your product or service.
- Define your position in the industry.
- Strategize your marketing efforts.

Core Competencies

A company's core competency is the one thing it can do better than any of its competitors. It is where its expertise lies and where it is essential for the company to be successful. It is also the company's "brand" and what it is known for.

A core competency can be a product, such as Microsoft being known for computer software, or for a service, such as FedEx being known for guaranteed on-time delivery.

You also have core competencies, although perhaps you have never defined them. It is imperative that you discover exactly where your expertise lies and what your "brand" will become known for. We will then discover what your features and benefits are, and that is exactly how one sells a product.

Defining Your Core Compentencies

Companies have attempted in recent years to move away from emotional or "gut instinct" hiring decisions to a method more quantifiable. The current trend in interviewing, behavioral interviews, looks for applicants with certain competency behaviors as these are believed to be the best predictors of success.

A competency is a skill or talent that makes the needed behavior seem almost effortless. Your core competencies will be those that are an always available resource for you to use, no matter what industry or situation.

Listed here are some of the more common competencies that are needed for working in the service industry:

High-octane energy	Leadership skills
Killer confidence	Listening skills
Engaging friendliness	Multitasking
Analytical ability	Organization
Communication skills	Planning ability
Customer service skills	Problem-solving
Delegation skills	Sales ability
Detail-oriented	Teamwork
Execution skills	Time-management skills
Flexibility	Work ethic

The competencies just mentioned are the 20 percent of the attributes that will get you 80 percent of the productivity.

These competencies, together with your powerful first impression, are what will make you irresistible to any hiring manager.

Pick out the few competencies that you *know* are your best and that you could utilize in any company anywhere. Base your decision on how you performed at a previous job or on a school project. These will be your core competencies.

Let's say that at your last job you worked as a crew chief on the front line at a fast-food restaurant, but because you were ambitious, you were also responsible for changing the ad every week in your store, which meant taking down all the old prices and point-of-sale materials.

And let's imagine you performed flawlessly on a consistent basis (execution skills), you led a team (teamwork) of rather inexperienced people (leadership skills), and delegated assignments (delegation skills) that had to get done before the ad-set deadline (time management).

In just our example alone, we demonstrated five skills that were needed on a consistent basis to achieve the desired goal, none of which are food-industry specific.

Using Your PAR

Another good way to think and describe about how you utilize your competencies is to use what's called a "PAR." PAR is an acronym for problem-action-result. Using a PAR allows you to tell a story about how you were presented with a problem, what action you took to solve it, and what the result was for the company.

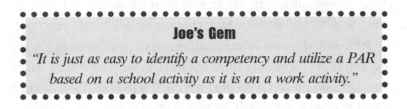

Joe's Gem

"It is just as easy to identify a competency and utilize a PAR based on a school activity as it is on a work activity."

If you now wanted to leave your fast-food job and apply to Circuit City for a customer-service associate position, I might ask you to "tell me about a time when you had to use your analytical and problem-solving skills at the fast food restaurant." It's possible you might respond to me with the following PAR:

"At ABC Fast Food, the front-counter associates had trouble getting customers to upgrade their regular meals to the king-size meals, which was causing the restaurant to not only miss its monthly sales goal of king-size meals, but to also loss out on additional profits (**P**roblem). As crew chief, I designed (analytical ability, problem-solving) and implemented (leadership skills) a fun and exciting incentive program (killer confidence) that allowed associates (teamwork) to focus on daily goals (sales ability), rather than monthly goals (**A**ction). This directly led to a 10-percent increase in the sale of king-size meals, as well as an increase in associate morale (**R**esult)."

Real Life

Rosa, the technology product specialist that I mentioned in an earlier chapter, had worked at a restaurant before she came to Circuit City. When I interviewed her, she described what she did on her job by stating that she was responsible for providing food service (customer service, engaging friendliness) at 15 tables (multitasking, high-octane energy) during the busiest hours of the day (execution skills). She was also expected to sell add-on sales (sales ability, killer confidence) of appetizers, drinks, and desserts, as well as get every customer order correct (detail-oriented) in as short a time as possible. Is it any surprise that Rosa was a star as a product specialist?

I would say you would be a pretty good candidate for the position, as our customer-service associates have to recommend products to our customers that they may not know they need. The fact that you had an awareness about the problem and then arrived at a satisfactory solution shows that you have what it takes to sell.

I interview many applicants from the fast-food industry and, as difficult a job as it is, there are numerous opportunities to discover how you use your competencies on a daily basis and how best to describe them for the job you want to get. It will take a little practice to uncover what they are and how to apply them for the job you are interviewing for, but after a short preparation you will be ready for an interview in any industry that crosses over.

Thinking Outside the Box

Whatever job you are currently at, you can break down what you do into competencies and see if they match up with the competencies or requirements for the job you want to get. If the job you want states that the applicant needs analytical skills, you want to provide an example or PAR that will illustrate what the problem was you encountered, how you analyzed and determined what action to take, and what the end result was.

Now that you know how to identify your competencies and how to turn them into a PAR or story, which is what they really are, you are ready to begin searching for a service-industry job outside the field you are currently in.

The government classifies service industry jobs into broad groups, and examples are listed here. It should also be pointed out that some of the jobs require specialized training:

- Arts and recreation (parks, athletic organizations).
- Auto industry (auto repair).
- Clerical and administrative (temps, maintenance, travel, landscaping).
- Communication (advertising companies).
- Educational services (private-school assistants, tutors).
- Entertainment industry (amusement parks).
- Finance (banking industry).
- Food-preparation industry (fast food and restaurants).
- Food stores (grocery and convenience stores).
- Hospitality industry (hotels, cleaning services).
- Information services (libraries).

- Mass-market retail (all-encompassing superstores).
- Personal services (beauty salons, parking valet, car wash).
- Retail sales (electronic and clothing stores).
- Social services (childcare).
- Specialty stores (bookstores and coffee shops).
- Transportation (trucking, courier services).
- Waste management (garbage and recycle collection).

A PAR will work for you regardless of the type of work you are currently doing. You may have to dig a little deeper to discover what special competency you use, but I am confident that you will surprise yourself in a short period of time.

Never narrow your focus to a job you "think" you can get. Your killer confidence will help create your powerful first impression that will allow you to interview as if the job is already yours. Always be prepared to give a PAR to show how your competency crosses over to the job you want to get.

How to Catch the Big One

It's no secret that you can have the best fishing line and tackle and still come home empty-handed (as I often do). Unless you put your hook into waters filled with hungry fish, there will never be a feeding frenzy. Part of getting a service-industry job is knowing where the schools of hungry fish are.

Now that you have identified some of your competencies, how do you find the hungry fish? There are currently so many ways to apply for a job that it can get mighty confusing just knowing what to do. However, to get the job you want in today's market, you must learn how to stand out from the crowd.

What's Your "It" Factor?

Have you ever thought about how an actor actually gets cast for a play or movie? What is that special ingredient—the "it" factor—that allows him or her to be the one chosen for the part from among hundreds of others?

I mentioned earlier that an actor has just a few minutes to catch the casting director's eye and gain his attention. How does an actor read the same lines as everyone else, but still be able to stand out?

The answer is that each actor must have a "brand," or a method of acting that is unique to him or her. They need something that the previous, and the following, 100 people auditioning for the part cannot duplicate. This is similar to the "wow" factor that companies attempt to portray to differentiate themselves in the crowded, competitive world of business.

You also must have a brand unique to yourself if the interviewer is going to see your "it" factor. You must answer the same questions that many applicants before and after you have answered in a way that allows you—and your brand—to stand out, so that you can get the job that you want.

Features and Benefits

In order to brand yourself and stand out in the industry, you must think of yourself as a product. Your "it" factor is what is special about you, but how can we best quantify it? What if you thought about yourself as a television?

In your ABC Fast Food PAR example earlier, you just took your core competencies (of which I counted six) and used them to describe your PAR, which is actually part of your features and benefits.

In any sales business, many customers do not really care about a product's features—all they care about are the benefits to them. If you were selling a television, it would be important to explain to a customer the difference between an analog television and a digital television. Some customers may want you to go into great detail about how a digital television has more lines of resolution and less visible scan lines than an analog television (feature), but other customers may only care that the digital television features give superior picture quality than the analog television (benefit).

The same applies to your brand. Your "features" are your competencies, which may not mean anything but an empty statement to the interviewer. For example, being "customer-focused" (feature) does not say much about what you would do for the company if hired.

However, saying that your company had a product return rate of 12 percent, and that by utilizing your analytical skills to identify the problem of poor associate knowledge, you designed a customer-service training program that developed the associates' empathy and listening skills to cut down returns to 8 percent (benefit) says a lot about what you could do for the interviewer's company if hired.

Strategic Search Style

I have discovered throughout my years of retail interviewing that applicants seem to fall into one of two style categories when job searching (generic and branded) and it's important to know what category you would place yourself, as that determines how you search for a company to work for.

I've listed several characteristics of both applicant search styles on the following page. It is not unusual for an applicant to have a few characteristics from both generic and branded styles.

Generic	Branded
Weak first impression	Powerful first impression
High-risk tolerant	Low-risk tolerant
Changes job for no reason	Changes job for opportunity
Erratic work history	Stable work history
Nonindustry specific	Industry specific
May have quit previous job	May have lost previous job
No minimum job requirements	Minimum job requirements
Unprepared for interview	Prepared for interview

Most service-industry applicants fall into the generic group, and many are either students or those out of school who have no current career goals. Branded group applicants tend to be more professional, with either managerial or highly trained skills, or are recent graduates with a defined career goal.

Generic Applicants

Generic applicants are the brown-paper-bag candidates of the interviewing world. If you see yourself in this category, good luck getting noticed. You more than likely blend in and get lost with the pool of applicants that interviewed before you, as well as those coming in behind you, similar to the way your meat, potatoes, and vegetables run together at a greasy-spoon restaurant. If hiring managers do remember you, it will be because of the long hair or strange-looking clothes.

If you fit the qualities of a generic applicant, you are high-risk tolerant, meaning that you can take a chance on changing jobs just for the sake of changing jobs. This is probably why you may be one of those who seem to have a history of jumping jobs every three to six months—it's because you can.

It's possible that you can be out of work for an extended period because you either live at home with your parents or you have another way to sustain yourself. It often appears as if it's no big deal if you work.

When I interview a generic applicant, there seems to be less drive to either get the job or even care about where he or she works. This individual is usually out looking because he needs a few bucks for school or, worse, his parents are pushing him to work. He could be working anywhere, and that feeling often comes across in the interview. Jerry, a fellow Store Director with Circuit City, validates that point when he states that "many applicants I interview act like they don't want to be here." How true.

Because of the high-risk tolerance, generic applicants usually have a history of job-hopping (they quit their job whenever things become boring or don't go their way). I have known many associates who will either quit or threaten to quit if they cannot get a night they need off, say, for a rock concert.

If you are a generic applicant, your manner of job search is a little less precise, very often filling out applications haphazardly to several types of businesses in the hope that one of them sticks. Because employment is not a major concern, you have minimal job requirements regarding pay, paid time off, and benefits. You may be more concerned with the work schedule and having flexibility to get days off.

This ultimately leads to the detrimental job history of decreasing pay or responsibility, rather than showing an increase in each, almost as if you are running away from something.

Think back to when you wanted something so badly that you would do almost anything to get it. What was that drive, that feeling, and where did you get it?

This is what's missing in a generic applicant. The drive and the passion that says that she wants the job and that she is the perfect candidate for it.

It is extremely unlikely that you can ever have a powerful first impression as a generic applicant, because you will always have a low PFI Index (high-octane energy, killer confidence, and engaging friendliness will all be in short supply).

You will probably arrive unprepared for the interview due to your lack of motivation. Thus, it may take you many interviews to get a job, which in turn may cause you to go for extended periods without working.

Branded Applicants

If you are a branded applicant, congratulations—you are the platinum card of the interviewing industry. Interviewers will be on a first-name basis with you as they both remember and talk about your potential with other members of management.

Branded applicants are low-risk tolerant and take a big chance when changing jobs. These applicants cannot afford to be out of work for an extended period due to demands on their income, such as a mortgage, a family, or school. They also have more to lose if they make a mistake in choosing the wrong company to move to. Thus, they normally will have a stable job history.

When I interview branded applicants, they will offer a motivated reason for wanting to work at my company. They are versed in the demands of retail and have the required confidence that they will succeed.

Among these candidates, the majority is currently employed (or may have recently lost a job), have a stable job history, and are looking for a better job with more pay. Many times the more experienced candidates are looking for an advancement opportunity they may not have at their current (or previous) job.

If you are a branded job applicant, your job search is much more precise, with resumes sent to specific businesses within your industry, or one in which you are attempting to break into. You may network amongst your industry relationships or apply online at specific companies you desire to work for.

You always have minimum job requirements such as pay, paid time off, and full-time benefits. Because you are always looking to improve yourself, seldom will you take a cut in pay or responsibility.

It is extremely likely that you create a powerful first impression as a branded applicant as your high PFI Index shows you have the necessary high-octane energy, killer confidence, and engaging friendliness.

Whether or not you can quickly get a job depends greatly upon the industry you are in, or trying to break into.

What Type of Applicant Are You?

What group would you place yourself in after reading the previous descriptions? Chances are that if you are searching for an entry-level, service-industry job, you are a generic style applicant. This probably does not bode well for your job future unless you can make some quick changes.

Here's one quick change you can make: Always interview as if you are a branded applicant! If you have a powerful first impression, even if you have a few of the generic group characteristics, you will most likely come off as a branded candidate.

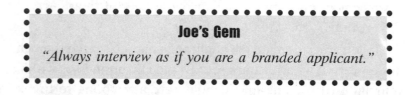

Joe's Gem

"Always interview as if you are a branded applicant."

Positioning

Every new business must confront the idea of positioning at one time or another. Positioning is where a company sees its niche in the industry, and where its products and services fit into the marketplace.

Positioning determines where the company will concentrate on building its brand and where it will spend its marketing resources. Positioning also looks at the company's competitors to determine where there is an opportunity to create or take market share, as well as discover its uniqueness.

You must also position yourself as to where in the industry you would have the greatest opportunity to create a powerful first impression and get the job you want. You must discover your defining characteristics of your brand and determine where they would it be utilized. What sector of the service industry would be best served by your "features and benefits"? You can do this by doing the following:

- Identifying your core competencies.
- Using your PAR stories to identify your features and benefits.

Emotional Hiring

I would be doing you a disservice if I led you to believe that competencies are the greatest thing going in the interviewing world. As much as career counselors will say that competencies are everything, and many interviewers may not admit it, hiring managers *do* make emotional hiring decisions, as I previously mentioned.

The good news for you is that there will be times that, all things being equal, the person with the powerful first impression will get the job offer. There are thousands of small companies and sole proprietorships whose hiring managers have never heard of a competency or seen a perfect resume. These are businesspeople who have been successful for many years and pride themselves on being able to spot talent using just their gut instinct.

If you interviewed with one of these businesspeople and were able to demonstrate with a powerful first impression how a few (20 percent) of your competencies (communications skills, work ethic, sales ability) could impact a large part (80 percent) of his business (sales, customer service), there is no question you would be a candidate for the position.

To use another football analogy, there are very few job-interview techniques more scientific and quantifiable than the National Football League (NFL) scouting combine. It is here that teams from the NFL hold a three-day interview to test every imaginable attribute that a college football player can have.

Millions of dollars will have already been spent scouting, charting, and watching tape of every player under draft consideration before management actually gets to spend time with the player. The player competencies needed are speed, agility, strength, range of motion, balance, cardiovascular endurance, and so on. There are, of course, even psychological tests.

My point is that even after spending millions, and observing and testing the top college players in the world at their positions during a period of three days, team management will often make their draft decision on an emotional basis, because sometimes the differences between the players are so small that it really comes down to who will be best athlete for the team.

This is what you must convince the hiring manager of the company you are applying to: that *you* are the best player for his or her team (and then be able substantiate the reasons why by using a PAR).

It's finally time to identify and do research on the companies you think you may want to work for. Who wants to be a Web wizard?

Chapter 6

Become a Private Eye:

Doing the Homework

The actor struggles against insurmountable odds, always searching for that one role, that one part that will separate him from the rest, define him as a performer, and give him what every actor longs for: a career.

One of the first interview questions I always ask applicants is why they want to work at Circuit City. I can usually tell from this question alone the applicant's motivation for being there in front of me. Is she there out of desperation because she needs a job and it wouldn't matter what company she was interviewing with, or is there a genuine reason why she wants to work for my company?

It always amazes me how many answer by either giving me a blank stare, or by having absolutely no clue as to why they want to work for us or what we are all about. If I were an applicant and wanted to make a powerful first impression, that would be the first thing I would focus on.

Real Life

I asked Ritchie, an applicant for a product-specialist position, what interested him in Circuit City. "I don't know. I never really thought about it," he said. "Then it wouldn't matter to you if we were sitting here now in the middle of a competitor's store, would it?" I countered. Ritchie didn't hesitate as he gave a shrug of the shoulders. "No, I guess not," he said. I never heard if the competition hired him.

Know Your Motivation

An actor must know his character's inner motivation to play a convincing role. We have all seen great movies with acting performances where the actor is so believable that he or she *is* the character. This is the type of performance you will need to portray in the interviewer's office in order to get the job that you want.

In the world of screenwriting, motivation is king! Every great screenplay is built upon the motivation of the main character, or protagonist, and we in the audience are right there with him or her.

Without motivation, we do not have Luke Skywalker risking his life to save Princess Leia from the Empire in *Star Wars*.

Without motivation, we do not have Indiana Jones giving up the Holy Grail to save his father in *Indiana Jones and the Last Crusade*.

We all like to be flattered. I was once a writing tutor while I was in college, and I would often have students come to me to have me help them write their psychology papers. There were several writing tutors they could have gone to, as well as the school's writing center. Why did they come to me?

My specialty was in cranking out the papers on short notice. Students would often wait until days (and sometimes hours) before a research paper was due, and come see me because they knew I was the king of speed. Often, I had little time to accommodate their request, but I usually did so just because the student had impressed me with his or her knowledge of my business.

Hiring Managers Are Human

This might come as a surprise, but hiring managers are human! I thoroughly enjoy hearing from applicants who say that they want to work at Circuit City, not because they need a job, but because their friend says what a great place it is to work. Or that every time they shop at my store it is such a pleasant experience that they want to be a part of it.

What kind of powerful first impression do you think you would make if you stated to me that you agreed with the company's mission statement and it was something you could get excited about? Or that you had read that Circuit City was a great turnaround story due to its impressive, past fiscal-year performance, and that you can see yourself becoming part of the management team in the future?

I would instantly think that you had initiative because you actually took the time to learn something about my business.

Web Wizard

Becoming a Web wizard is the first step in becoming a private eye. You must research the perspective company before going on an interview if you want to make the hiring manager feel that you know his company and his industry.

You'll discover that you can research a company in as little as 15 minutes and still make a powerful first impression. There is no need to overload yourself and feel overwhelmed with data from several sources when most service-industry hiring managers are pleasantly surprised when an applicant knows anything relevant about the company and industry.

Becoming a Web wizard is easy! I'll take you through a few company searches to gather enough data to make a powerful first impression. I'll also address how to track down some smaller, local companies that might not have a large Web presence.

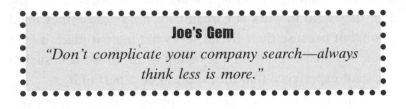

Joe's Gem

"Don't complicate your company search—always think less is more."

Know What You Are Looking For

If you are going to get the job that you want, it's obviously important that you know what information you are looking for so you know where to look. There are many reasons why you may want to work at a company besides money, of course, and each has its own strengths during the interview.

Know your motivation! The motivation that is important to you will say something about who you are and will also contribute to your powerful first impression. This is not something you just want to memorize for the interview, but rather something that you believe in. The more genuine your motivation, the more believable your performance.

The information is also a must to know in order to be prepared should you receive a phone call from a telephone screener at an unexpected time. It is difficult to prepare for this gatekeeper, because you are normally taken by surprise. Although most service-industry jobs will not screen by telephone, it is always best to be prepared.

To help you identify your inner motivation and prepare you for this important question, I've listed here several of the reasons why you may be considering working for the company of your choice:

- **You agree with the company's mission statement and guiding principles.** This is always a great place to start. Companies pride themselves on their mission statements. Some examples are companies that will not do business in countries that exploit minors or pay slave wages, companies that will not produce products that are not environmentally friendly, and companies that believe in giving back to the community.

- **There is good opportunity for advancement.** Companies love young people who say that they are interested in supervisory or managerial positions. It usually shows an applicant has initiative, has a desire to develop, and plans to be with the company for a long time.

- **The company revenues show a history of growth.** This shows that a company is not only growing its business, but may also be developing new opportunities within the company by developing new markets, opening new stores, or creating new positions.

- **The company has excellent benefits.** This is probably more important to you than the employer, and it is often not advisable to list as a primary motivation. However, if you are a student, and the company you are considering features tuition reimbursement as a benefit, it is a good secondary reason to want to work there. Companies take great pride in furnishing tuition reimbursement, especially for part-timers. This also sends a message to the interviewer that you plan on being with the company at least until the time you are out of school.

- **The company is an industry leader.** Everyone wants to work for a leader. There is a smug satisfaction in working for the number-one company in an industry, whether it be in fast food, office supplies, or apparel.

- **You are a frequent customer of the business.** Companies love applicants who are customers. It demonstrates that you are familiar with its products, have already interacted with the store associates, and probably have a good idea of what it takes to work there. If the business is in the food industry, you can also talk about the greatness of the food and what your favorite dish is.

- **You have heard from a friend that the business is a great place to work.** Nothing is more influential than being referred by another associate. Most hiring managers trust that their own associates know what it takes to work there and will only recommend those who will be successful. Companies also want associates to enjoy and have fun in the workplace, and nothing does that better than hiring one's friend.

- **You have a strong desire to learn and gain more experience in that type of business.** I always enjoy hearing from young-adult applicants, especially students, who are looking to go into business as a career and see my company as a training ground for learning how that world operates. It's also a good rapport-builder, as it allows you the opportunity to ask intelligent questions about the necessary ingredients for great customer service and sales.

- **You see the company as the type of business where you can utilize your talents.** This is a great opportunity for you to lay the foundation of what competencies you have before the interviews really gets heated up. If you've observed the company associates in action, and even spoken to a few, you can usually tell what some of the needed competencies are. This allows you to say why you would do a great job and, more importantly, what it would contribute to the hiring manager's business.

- **You are looking to fill a seasonal or temporary employment position the company is hiring for.** This can sometimes be the absolute best way to get into the company of your choice. Always remark that you would like to stay on with the company if your performance warrants it. I cannot remember the last time I laid off a seasonal associate who was an exceptional performer. There is not enough talent walking through my door to allow me to lose a player when there is a real possibility of losing three associates the following week due to the industry turnover rate.

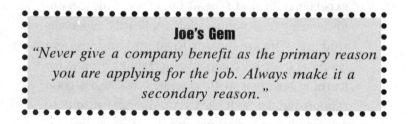

Joe's Gem

"Never give a company benefit as the primary reason you are applying for the job. Always make it a secondary reason."

There's No Place Like Home

You have identified some of the companies you would like to work for in the previous chapter. Now that you have your prospects, the first place you would start is the home page of the company's Website. Nearly every major company has a careers section that will normally list its mission statement, guiding principles, career path, benefits, and so on.

Joe's Gem

"Always check a company's Website for its mission statement and guiding principles first to see if you agree with them."

You always want to check the mission statement and guiding principles first to see if you agree with them—just in case. If you are interested in progressing into management, you'll want to discover if the company is experiencing sales growth while doing your Web search, and if there could possibly be future opportunities for advancement.

If you need specific benefits, such as tuition reimbursement, you'll want to look into that also. Also check any company press releases, history of the company, and so on, even though it may not all be relevant to your job search. It's good to keep in mind that no company will likely put negative information on its Website, so you should always do a brief search of at least *Hoover.com* and *Google.com* to look for any recent, pertinent news.

One-page Search

Your goal should be to do a one-page search on every company you plan on interviewing with. You will have all the pertinent information you will need in less than 15 minutes to confidently state to an interviewer why you are interested in the company.

The scenario we will use for our purposes is that you are a college student who has little retail experience. Your plans are to work at a company that has tuition reimbursement because you intend on staying with the company at least until you complete your education in two years. You would like an employer with flexible work hours and to have it offer an opportunity for you to be developed and challenged.

We'll quickly look at the Websites of four national companies for the following information, which was current as of January 2006:

- Mission statement or guiding principles.
- Tuition-reimbursement benefit.
- Job-description competencies.
- Company-revenue growth.
- Recent pertinent business news.

You'll finalize the company search by identifying what competencies will probably be needed based on the job description provided on the company Website, as well as what kind of experience would be helpful.

Barnes & Noble

Industry:

- Music, video, and books

Guiding principles and mission statement:

- Determined to be the best bookseller in the business
- Operate the best specialty retail business in America
- Be a credit to the community

Tuition-reimbursement benefit:

- Yes

General job description:

- Provide a friendly, casual, helpful experience for the customer

- Know product; keep product organized, inviting, and well-stocked
- Pride themselves on fast cashiering
- Authorize returns and exchanges
- Ensure lines move fast and never get long

Company revenue growth:

- One-year sales growth (18.1%)
- Recent growth—holiday 2005 sales increase 5.2% from holiday 2004

Recent pertinent business news:

- None

Required competencies:

- Energetic; customer friendly; detailed; multitasking; love of books; decision-making; passionate

Helpful experience:

- Cashiering; visual merchandising; customer service

Circuit City

Industry:

- Consumer electronics

Guiding principles and mission statement:

- Always provide our customers with an enjoyable experience that they would tell a friend about
- Greet and be available to every customer; smile and be friendly
- Share our enthusiasm and product knowledge
- Let our customers know that we're glad to serve them

Tuition-reimbursement benefit:

- Yes

General job description:
- Dedicated to industry leading customer satisfaction
- Dedicated to ensuring customers have the best shopping experience possible
- Friendly, knowledgeable, and energetic product specialists, customer service and warehouse associates

Company revenue growth:
- One year sales growth 7.5%
- Recent growth - record December 2005 sales increase 12.1% from December 2004

Recent pertinent business news:
- None

Required competencies:
- Energetic; customer friendly; passionate; love of electronics, music, and movies

Helpful experience:
- Customer service; sales

Starbucks

Industry:
- Specialty eateries

Guiding principles and mission statement:
- Provide a great work environment and treat each other with respect and dignity
- Embrace diversity as an essential component in the way we do business
- Apply the highest standards of excellence to the purchasing, roasting, and fresh delivery of our coffee
- Develop enthusiastically satisfied customers all of the time

- Contribute positively to our communities and our environment

Tuition-reimbursement benefit:

- Yes

General job description:

- Commitment to excellence
- Emphasis on respect in how we treat our customers and each other
- Dedication to social responsibility
- Adaptable, self-motivated, passionate, and creative team players

Company revenue growth:

- One-year sales growth 20.3%
- Recent growth - January 2006 sales increase 10.0% from January 2005

Recent pertinent business news:

- Plans to open 700 U.S. stores in 2006

Required competencies:

- Energetic; customer friendly; adaptable; passionate

Helpful experience:

- Customer service

Red Lobster

Industry:

- Casual-dining restaurant

Guiding principles and mission statement:

- Make each guest feel special
- Have an overriding goal to be the best at what we do
- Be a positive influence in any community we're a part of

- Delight with little pleasures, such as remembered names and constant courtesies
- Always add energy, and be active, positive, and competitive

Tuition-reimbursement benefit:

- Yes

General job description:

- Make every single soul feel welcome at the door
- Greet and seat guests and always invite them back
- Provide efficient service by guiding guests through menus, while suggestively selling

Company revenue growth:

- One-year sales growth 5.5%
- Recent growth - January 2006 sales increase 6.3% from January 2005

Recent pertinent business news:

- None

Required competencies:

- Energetic; customer friendly; passionate

Helpful experience:

- Customer service; sales

All of the previous information was gathered from multiple sites in less than 15 minutes per company. Of course, you can spend more time on each site, and I highly recommend it if it is a company you are seriously considering.

One-page Analysis

I chose four national, highly regarded companies in different industries, with the smallest company having more than 600 locations, that nearly every reader would be familiar with.

A few items should immediately jump out:

* All four companies have some form of tuition reimbursement.

* All four companies have experienced recent growth.

* The competencies required for all four companies curiously include energetic, passion, and customer friendly—or what I call an above-average PFI Index.

Based on our one-page search scenario, all four companies would be excellent choices for your employment because your need of tuition reimbursement would be satisfied. Although I didn't list flexibility and development in my detailed company analysis, it was evident from the Websites that it certainly appeared to be the case at all four.

Is it surprising to see that all of the companies had as a required competency high-octane energy (energetic), killer confidence (passion), and engaging friendliness (customer-friendly)? Do you think you would get the job you want if you entered the interview with a powerful first impression?

Although I recommended that it would be helpful to have sales or customer experience at a few of the businesses, it would probably not be necessary if you were able to convince the hiring manager that you had many of the necessary competencies and could quickly be trained.

Local Companies

Most smaller, local companies will have little Web presence, if any at all. A search for a few local companies here in Salt Lake City either shows no Website or one with limited information.

Several restaurants had Websites with limited use that used the site to show their menus and, in some instances, allowed me to order food for delivery or pickup. Even a company with multiple locations only used the site to display its products and prices, although it was possible to submit a job application.

This shouldn't come as a surprise to you. A company normally does not have detailed associate-guiding principles or a written mission statement unless it is a large corporation. The owner may still have his or her own personal beliefs, but has just not taken the steps to outline them into an official document.

This makes a visit to the company more important to research the needed information and to observe the associates in action to determine what kind of competencies are needed. Chances are good that, no matter what business you went to, it would require a powerful first impression to get the job you want.

Now that you're a Web wizard, let's look into whether or not a resume is in your future.

Chapter 7

History Lesson:

To Resume or Not to Resume

The actor realizes that his headshot and a few bad plays are his resume—his body of work. But, if he let that define his career, fame would never be his. So, he continues utilizing his contacts to generate referrals, to audition for any role, however small, and discover that fresh character that is inside himself to find success.

I don't use resumes! There, I said it. I have never hired an associate based on a resume, and I don't know if I ever will. The resume, at its best, can be the perfect calling card to get you an interview. However, at its worst, the resume can lead you to a quick trip to the trash can.

An impressive, well-written resume generates panache and instant credibility similar to shopping at Nordstrom and pulling out the ultra-platinum card. It might make the buyer feel good, but the store also takes cash.

Be the Fresh Face

Sometimes a sitcom producer is looking for that fresh face rather than the one who had the lead in *Macbeth*. *You are that fresh face!* Maybe you have no job history or have just worked at a few fast-food joints, but you are still a resource to prospective employers. Your resume is another step in your audition preparation but, if used, it is imperative that it be designed in such a way that it will present you with a powerful first impression.

Imagine that you are an actor sending in your "headshot" to be considered for the latest sitcom. What do you think your chances would be if the photo was blurry or grainy, or just looked cheap—as if it was taken at a one-minute photo studio?

Because the casting agent is going to spend just seconds glancing at your photo, chances are there is no way you could have "the look" that he or she was searching for because the photo did not do you justice.

It would not matter how great your acting ability. You would not get the audition call because of the headshot.

Resume First Impressions

This is what can happen with your resume. Your resume is your "headshot," and the hiring manager will probably spend just as little time looking at it as the casting agent.

Todd Bermont, in his best-selling book *10 Insider Secrets to a Winning Job Search*, states that your resume is your very own advertisement. Bermont says one gets only 15 seconds to make a positive first impression, or you simply don't have a chance!

Only 15 seconds? Are you kidding me? What hiring manager, or worse, what gatekeeper can analyze a resume and validate a candidate's worth in less time than it takes to watch a Coke commercial? Sadly, I have to agree with Bermont's assessment. It either does the trick and you get the phone call, or it doesn't and you ended up wasting some good paper.

I am looking at a professional online resume service right now that says hiring managers spend only 10 seconds reviewing each resume before making a decision. 10 seconds! But for $199, the service will create a resume for a workplace neophyte. I don't know about you, but that sounds like a lot of shifts at McDonalds to me.

Death of the Resume

A search of *Amazon.com* under the word *resume* yields over 1,800 book results! Go into any bookstore and I know it *seems* that there are that many. I think the time has come that we have to ask ourselves just how many different ways is there to write a resume.

And it's not just books. There are numerous Websites, resume-writing services, and school career-counseling centers. But one fact remains: Young adults still cannot get jobs!

The job statistics quoted in a previous chapter are made all the more remarkable when one realizes that the young people of today have more job resources available to them than at any time in history, but they are still losing the jobs to the immigrants and older folks.

The resume at one time held a competitive advantage for savvy job-seekers similar to an upstart business that develops a new technology. The resume was a calling card in the way a screenwriter presents a screenplay as evidence of his or her writing. It actually reflected the work of what the applicant had done and could hopefully replicate for his or her next company.

Iomega was a leader in the computer mass-storage industry with its Zip Drive, which allowed one to back up his or her huge files in a way the floppy disks never could. However, it lost its competitive advantage as other companies developed competing technologies, such as the rewriteable CD and Thumb Drive, and it has never recovered as a major player.

Now that the resume is as ubiquitous as a screenplay in Hollywood, that competitive advantage has been removed. Once the internet and electronic applications evolved, action words and keywords have become *de rigueur* to get into the electronic databases and get noticed by the headhunters and hiring managers. I think one has to ask this question: Is the resume still as effective as it once was, or is it nothing more than a dog and pony show to see who can have the best layout, design, writing, and so on?

Use Your Personal Power

I'm going to let you in on a secret. *You do not need a resume to get hired!* I think that bears repeating: You do not need a resume to get hired. Just as one can get acting auditions at casting calls without first sending in his "headshot," applicants have a great chance of bypassing the resume game altogether.

It is your high-octane energy, killer confidence, and engaging friendliness that the employer is looking for and that is now your calling card. *You* will create that powerful first impression and not words written on a piece of paper.

Can you feel the empowerment? You are responsible and in control for your getting the job. Would you rather be represented for 15 seconds by a static piece of paper, or be represented by your dynamic personality, where your personal power can shine?

I know writers who have written books for many years and have never sold one, yet they continually send query letters and proposals to agent and publishers hoping the next one gets the deal. If you are not familiar with the book-publishing world, the odds are enormously stacked against a first-time author to sell a book this way.

Joe's Gem

"Never, ever let a piece of paper do a job your own powerful first impression can do many times better."

When I began writing nonfiction, I also sent a few query letters to agents about a self-help book proposal that I had at the time even though I knew the odds for success were long. The response was always a polite rejection, stating that the book was a great idea, but the self-help field was crowded with so many others.

When I completed the proposal for the book you are reading, I vowed that I wouldn't let a piece of paper determine my future. I arranged to go to the Book Expo Event in New York City, where thousands of publishers sell their books to the booksellers and librarians, and personally introduced myself and my proposal to career book publishers. I handed my proposal to 12 publishers that weekend, all of whom listened to my passionate tale of why this book should be published and why I was the person to write it.

I received three publication offers within a week, which was an amazing success rate, and one that probably would not have happened had I just sent the proposal in cold to the company headquarters rather than use my powerful first impression!

References

Robin Ryan, in her book *Soaring on Your Strengths*, claims that the resume is not the most powerful tool in your career arsenal, but your references. I couldn't agree more.

Answer me this: Would you hire an interior decorator to make over your bedroom, a contractor to add a second story to your home, or a mechanic to rebuild your car's engine based off a resume that said extraordinary things about his performances? Or would you just check a few of his references to inspect the quality of his work?

Be careful about your references, however. *References* is a broad term that could possibly be taken negatively or positively. I am sometimes surprised when I receive a telephone call from a company asking for a reference check on a substandard associate who I would not rehire. I am required by Circuit City, due to possible legal exposure, to refer the caller to our employment-verification service. However, I always wonder why that specific associate used me as a reference when he or she must have known I was not pleased with his or her performance.

Always ask your references if they are comfortable being a reference for you and, more importantly, can make a recommendation on your behalf. Never let them get taken by surprise.

Joe's Gem

"Always ask your references if they are comfortable being a reference. Never let them get taken by surprise."

Use Power Referrals

Nothing creates a powerful first impression as a power referral does. Never confuse a referral with a reference, although the word *refer* is the root of each word. You'll learn in the next chapter how a power referral can double your chances to get you an interview that may have been impossible, especially one that is in what recruiters call the "hidden" job market. Without question, I consider a power referral as the number one way to staff my store.

Imagine that a new Mexican restaurant has opened by your school or business and you went to try it out on your lunch. A friend asks you upon your return how the place was. Here are a couple of different replies you could give if you weren't totally displeased with the experience:

1. It wasn't bad. I had the steak burrito smothered in enchilada sauce. It wasn't the best I've had, but I'd probably go back again.

Not a bad referral—you'll probably check the place out just to see if you have a different reaction, and because most of us like to try new restaurants.

2. Oh god, you've got to go there. The steak burrito
    was out of this world! Be sure to get it smothered
    in enchilada sauce; they just load on the cheese
    and sour cream!

Where do you think your friend will be going to eat the
very next time he or she goes to lunch? This is a power referral. In the job-hunter world, this is the difference between a
reference (a hiring manager calling a reference) and a power
referral (a power referral calling a hiring manager). Reaction
number two is what every business strives for. It is a leverage
point for your use to create a powerful first impression during
your first few minutes.

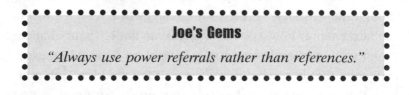

Joe's Gems

"Always use power referrals rather than references."

They Want to Turn You Down

Richard Nelson Bolles, in his classic book *What Color Is
Your Parachute?*, states that the job-hunter's preferred method
of job searching is to use a resume and get invited in for an
interview. Unfortunately, that is exactly the employer's *least
preferred* method of hiring. Whereas the applicant sees his or
her job hunt and resume as a hiring game, the employer sees it
as an elimination game.

Your service-industry resume is only a reason to turn you
down! It will not get you an interview in most circumstances.

As mentioned earlier, most of the larger retail companies have now gone to electronic applications and will call you in for an interview based on that alone. Most smaller, proprietor businesses will normally have you just do an application and not even ask for a resume.

I receive resumes only after an applicant is called in for an interview and brings one with him or her as Circuit City requires an online application before being considered. Based on my experience, nine times out of 10 the resume will look amateurish (with spellings errors, poor layout, and poor design). And the other 10 percent will be nothing to brag about, either. Chances are that if I went entirely by what I saw on the resume, I would end the interview and send the applicant on his or her way.

The food industry is another segment that doesn't ask for a resume. Research of mine has indicated that the majority of businesses only require one to fill out an application. (Because this industry is heavily franchised, many of the companies require that you go into the restaurant, rather than apply online.)

Resume Required

I realize the resume is still required for most management and specialized jobs. Also, if one is going to apply online at the job banks, such as *Monster.com* and *Hotjobs.com*, a resume is normally needed. There are even a few perks in doing this. Currently, when you post your resume on *Monster.com* you double your chances to get the job as compared to those who don't post their resumes, according to their statistics. Imagine that! Maybe it means that the hiring managers spend 20–30 seconds checking your resume out!

You've hopefully agreed with everything I've said up until now. You've bagged your old resume and gone out into the business world to rightfully claim your job. You've sent in some electronic applications and filled out a few paper ones. You've maybe even done a little networking and—guess what—a friend turns you on to a business that you would love to work at, but the manager wants a resume. What's the first thing you do before you panic (or even after you panic)?

Resume Madness

There are as many ways today to create a resume as there are ways to prepare chicken. Do you use a chronological or functional resume? What exactly do you put in it? What do you do if you have many instances of job-hopping?

We've talked much about competencies and what *you* can do for the company you are applying at, so it makes sense to start there.

Real Life

I interviewed David for an entertainment-product specialist position. David had all the powerful first impression that one could ever want in an associate. He was one of those applicants that I had to pinch myself when I saw him because I could not believe I was lucky enough to have this guy walk through my door. He was a high-octane individual who had it all going for him, such as volunteering and extra-school activities. To top it off, he was one of those individuals I rarely see: someone who knows what they're doing tomorrow and in five years. I scanned his resume as we chatted for a minute or two. It was not very

> original, and it was also poorly thought out and executed.
> It was the kind of resume that would get an applicant turned
> down without getting an interview. But here was this guy, a
> future superstar in the business world, sitting in front of
> me. Yeah, I trusted the powerful first impression, and David
> was a great hire who has now gone on to bigger things.

Robin Kessler and Linda A. Strasburg, authors of the timely *Competency-Based Resumes*, offer a great resource on how to design the competency-based resume that's right for you. The authors substantiate the claim that you need to position yourself differently than you have in the past to compete and win with employers today. They add that effective interviewing is based on the assumption that past behavior is the best predictor of future behavior.

Kessler and Strasburg outline the four key elements of a competency:

- **Written description.** What are the most accurate words that clearly describe your competency?
- **Measurable work.** Measurable is the success rate of the work you achieved, such as "increased sales by 30 percent within one year." Measurable work includes something quantifiable: an amount, percentage, or time involved to complete the work.
- **Habits and skills.** What are your key habits and skills? Make sure the same word used as a competency is also used in the written description of your skill and habit.

- ◆ **To achieve a work objective.** What did you accomplish? The outcome or effect of your work is important. Ask how your work saved time or money, or improved the process. How did it benefit the organization?

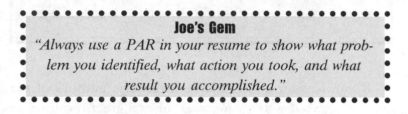

Joe's Gem

"Always use a PAR in your resume to show what problem you identified, what action you took, and what result you accomplished."

You should always include competencies that play to your strengths. Marcus Buckingham and Donald Clifton, in their book *Now, Discover Your Strengths,* portray a fascinating picture of how each of us deals with our world in an unique way.

The authors help us identify our strengths and offer advice on how to leverage them for powerful results both in our lives and on the job. I highly recommend that you learn what your strengths are so that you may fully exploit them for your success.

A Resume's Powerful First Impression

If you are going to use a resume to get the job you want, it must create a powerful first impression within seconds, similar to a perfect photo. Bump your resume to the following list to validate that you have the necessary ingredients that ensure it will be examined for your competencies and not just thrown in the trash:

- ◆ Professional-quality resume paper.
- ◆ Appropriate style font.

- Perfect black ink.
- Business-appropriate e-mail address.
- Traditional style layout.
- No drawings, pictures, or symbols that could be taken as "weird."
- No misspelled words or incorrect grammar.

If your resume is seen as the bad "headshot," you'll be turned down in an instant, and it won't matter a whit what kind of competencies you have—you'll never get the phone call for the audition.

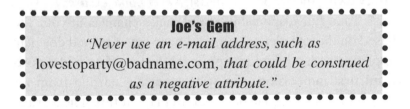

Joe's Gem

"Never use an e-mail address, such as lovestoparty@badname.com, *that could be construed as a negative attribute."*

Jon Reed and Rachel Myers, in their book *Resumes From Hell*, eloquently show what *not* to put in a resume. Even though most of it is common sense, this can sometimes be useful if you are still new to the world of resumes.

It can be used as a checklist to see if you have anything just as crazy in your resume, such as the one guy who wrote that in his spare time he likes to work on his computer and do various activities with his girlfriend. The resumes would be laugh-out-loud funny if there wasn't a little sadness because the stories were true.

Your Past

It is imperative to remember that whatever kind of resume you create, it is nothing more than a history book. To paraphrase an Anthony Robbins quote that one's past does not equal one's future tells you everything you need to know. A resume is nothing except a record of your *past*! It says what you did up until the moment it was created (before you knew how to digitize your mind).

Whether you have no work history or a poor job history does not matter if you learned something from it (behavioral interviewing theory be damned!). *Never make excuses for your past*! Take full responsibility and make changes in your life based on the knowledge gained. I have never turned down an applicant with a limited or poor job history if he had a powerful first impression, can state what he learned from his past, and why things will be different in the future if he worked for me.

Experience

I guess I've really touched on what bothers me about resumes! It is a backward-looking document, rather than a forward-looking document. As stated earlier, it states where you've been rather than where you are going.

There is also a little bit of arrogance in me (something I believe every hiring manager should have a dose of) that asks the question of why I should turn down an applicant because of a previous job *where perhaps the management was terrible?* Of course, I'm giving you the benefit of the doubt here—maybe you *were* the problem.

I always ask my subordinate managers certain questions before we terminate anyone's employment due to poor performance. Did we do everything possible as leaders to produce and deserve a productive associate? Did we give him or her the training and the tools to succeed? Did we motivate, inspire, and reward him or her to succeed?

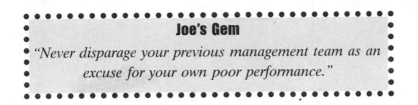

Joe's Gem

"Never disparage your previous management team as an excuse for your own poor performance."

Every time a hiring manager turns down an applicant because of his job history, and does so without validating, he or she is are making a decision based on another manager's performance. But if the service industry is not known for having the best-trained managers, doesn't that seem a little harsh? If you are a young person who has a history of leaving fast-food restaurants every three months, are you the problem, or is your teenage supervisor? It's something worth thinking about.

Applying Yourself

Now that you are relieved a resume is not needed, let's discover how you can apply yourself so you can finally get some interviews—and a job!

Chapter 8

Getting Backstage:

Finding and Applying for the Job

Nothing gives greater enjoyment to the actor than reading for a role that is new to anything he has ever done, no matter how small, and then taking the writer's words and speaking them as if they were his own.

Nothing compares to being backstage at a concert or on the set of a movie. Excitement fills the air. People are running around everywhere, each on a mission with a job to do to make the project a success. And the after-performance parties are legendary—fun for all for a job well-done. However, if you are not a member of the cast or crew, you usually don't get to attend unless you know someone.

Strategic Search

You must now strategize your marketing efforts and job search in a manner that will give you the best positioning above your competitors. If you are looking for your first job, it is much easier to break into the fast-food industry than any other. This industry will also hire the most applicants under the age of 18.

Although there are probably some of you groaning upon reading this, there is absolutely nothing wrong with working in the fast-food industry. As I stated earlier, your job is nothing but a mechanism to pay your bills so you can pursue your goals and dreams.

If you already have job experience and can demonstrate some features and benefits, there are many opportunities available to you because finding companies that will be willing to capitalize on your talents will not be difficult.

Finding the Schools of Hungry Fish

Discovering where the schools of hungry fish are is the first step in getting the job you want. There are so many ways to find a job today that it is easy for one to get overwhelmed and not know where to begin. With so much conflicting information in books, on the Internet, and given by career counselors, how does someone with little job experience position himself to show off his brand?

You should have determined in a previous chapter exactly what is important to you and why you want to work at the company of your choice. This is different for everyone, but suffice it to say that most applicants are looking for the big one that will give them job experience, benefits, good pay, and opportunity.

Although it is unlikely that you will find a job that has everything you want early in your career, it is not impossible. Job searching is a journey that sometimes allows you to discover what you don't want in a job just as often as it allows you to discover what you do want. There is nothing wrong with accepting less in order to have an opportunity to learn more about yourself, change industries, and demonstrate that you have the competencies to achieve success in your new area. And there is no easier way to accomplish that goal than by announcing your intentions to the world.

It's Who You Know

You learned in a previous chapter that there is absolutely nothing more powerful than a power referral. This is the easiest way for you to get "backstage" in a company. A power referral is the ultimate in the world of referrals and literally doubles your chances to get the job you want, but it is important to understand that any associate referral increases your likelihood that you will at least get an interview.

A power referral is also the best way to crack what many in the career field call the hidden job market. These are the jobs that are not advertised in any way, but are openings waiting for the right person to fill them. *You* can be that right person! I recently lost two exceptional associates this past month to hidden jobs in their desired fields simply because they were able to get hired based on the power referrals they received.

Service-industry companies today are experiencing a great deal of turnover. In addition, associate morale is extremely low in most major companies. In fact, the norm in the retail industry is that, at any given time, 50 percent of the associates are considering another job.

Companies want associates to stay longer and be happier. Referred applicants carry greater weight because they are being referred by an associate who already knows the job expectations and whose opinion is valued.

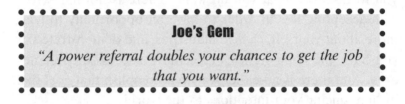

Joe's Gem

"A power referral doubles your chances to get the job that you want."

My associates also know what it takes to succeed in my store and business. Anytime one of them refers a candidate to me, I interview him or her no matter what his or her application looks like. Chances are the referred applicant also already knows the demanding hours, the necessity of selling, and the priority of customer service at my store.

If you are similar to most associates, you probably enjoy working with your friends and family because it creates a fun work atmosphere. Also, if you work amongst friends, typically you will stay longer at a job because you enjoy it more. Anytime I can hire a friend or family member of an associate I view it as a win-win situation in many ways. (Many companies also pay their associates for employee referrals, which creates even greater incentive for employees to recommend someone that they know.)

If you do not know anyone at the company where you want to work, do not let it discourage you. If it is a retail or food company in which the public interacts with the employees, it is very easy to strike up a conversation with one of the associates to question them about working at the business.

Visit the store for several weeks until you feel you know the employee well enough to ask if you can put him or her down as a reference on your application. Many referrals I get are customers who have met an associate in the store. Although the associate does not know the applicant personally, he or she will usually say that she has talked to him or her in the store and he or she seems to be a good person.

Real Life

I received an application from Greg for a product-specialist position. Greg listed Barb, a current product specialist in the store, as a referral. I questioned Barb about Greg's chances of working for us, and she stated that she didn't really know him, but that he was a customer who seemed like a nice guy and who came into the store every few days to recommend DVDs to his family and friends. I interviewed Greg based on Barb's comments and found him to be someone who really wanted to work for Circuit City. Greg also stated that he could offer the benefit of being able to help customers in the DVD department because he was so knowledgeable about movies. Greg took the initiative to double his chance to get the job he wanted and he was rewarded by being asked to join the team.

Networking

Why is it that when it comes to our job or career we feel that we have to go it alone, and that "networking" is a dirty word?

That asking someone for help or a lead is something difficult to do? Most of us dislike networking because of this.

I know that, for me, asking someone for help used to be one of the hardest things to do. I always felt I had to do everything on my own.

When I lived in Los Angeles, I would often watch the filming of sitcoms at the studios. Screenwriter friends of mine would get me into the shows and allow me to see their written words acted out just as they envisioned them. Afterwards, we would socialize with the cast and friends at the wrap parties.

I was a screenwriter at the time and, although I enjoyed the festive atmosphere, the parties allowed me to work the crowd and pitch my projects to any producers or agents who were there. After that failed, I would look for strangers who knew somebody, somewhere, who could further my interests.

Most of the time I struck out. But when I did get a name, I worked that connection until it led to a dead end, and then I shifted my energies elsewhere. I didn't know at the time that what I was doing was networking; I just saw it as survival.

Everyone jokes about the nepotism in Hollywood, and it's true, but it is not limited to relatives. I learned early on that Hollywood has high barriers to entry and that you have to know someone, anyone, who can turn you on to somebody who cares enough to help you get a break. Because without someone's help, you are one of thousands in the Hollywood food chain, and your chances for success, no matter how talented, are small.

The power of networking is that seldom does one forget who helped him or her, and it gives tremendous incentive to want to reciprocate and give someone else a break should you become successful and in a powerful enough position to do so.

Networking works in the interview because the more you know about an individual, the quicker you can build rapport and become friends. This is the basis behind career networking and why an applicant who is referred for a job has such a huge advantage over someone who is not.

This common bond enhances the opportunity for you to have a powerful first impression and allows both you and the interviewer to chat about your commonality for a minute or two, which does wonders to relieve any interview anxiety you may have.

Network While You Sleep

I am going to give you one of the most powerful networking tools you can ever use. Its effect is so strong that you can literally make contacts and get job referrals while you are asleep.

Perhaps at one time or another you experienced a friend who excitedly contacted you and said that she was thinking about you late last night and, knowing that you had recently broken up with your boyfriend, thought of a guy she knew that would be perfect for you to go out with.

You thanked her for thinking about you and wanting to set you up on the date, never stopping to realize that you went to bed early that night and what was happening was being done behind the scenes while you were sleeping.

The important thing to remember is this: No one will ever come up with a referral or idea for you if they do not know what you are looking for. It's that simple. The idea of networking while you sleep is so simple, yet the power in it multiples your efforts a hundredfold.

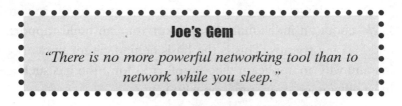

Joe's Gem

"There is no more powerful networking tool than to network while you sleep."

You *must* talk to your friends and family and let them know you are looking for a job, and what kind of employment you desire. You never know when someone who cares about you will encounter a situation where they will have an opportunity to drop your name to someone in a position of authority.

It even pays to speak with employees at the company you desire to work for, because you can never tell when an opening will arise, and it could be that you will be the first one the associate thinks of when her department experiences turnover.

This is good advice no matter what you are looking for. Friends of mine will often call me about ideas that contribute enormously to my writing, saying they thought of this great idea that I can use in my current book. Many, many times these ideas are thought of late at night when they are home taking it easy, have less on their mind—and I am soundly asleep.

Never let a fear of failure or ridicule prevent you from announcing your intentions to the world. Never be afraid to let everyone know what your goals and dreams are and that you would appreciate any help they can give. It will give you a warm feeling after a few favorable occurrences that people are looking out for you and working on your behalf while you are getting some much needed rest!

There are, of course, many other ways to job search in the service industry besides using networking. The following is a list of strategies I recommend that are presented in what I believe is their order of effectiveness.

Internships

Internships, such as at a zoo or museum, are a great place to get work experience, especially if you are just beginning your career. Companies that offer internships are more willing to accept applicants with limited experience. An internship can also develop into a permanent job because you have already proven yourself.

School Career Centers

Job opportunities at school career centers are great if, naturally, you attend the school and can work at the companies that the school has developed a relationship with. Many times you can get a position that closely aligns with your major or area of interest. It is also possible to get an internship where you may only get college credit at first, but it may develop into a future position with the company.

These jobs usually pay a little more than the typical service-industry job, and the company is often a little more flexible on the required hours. Sometimes your school career counselor will know a contact in the company, which can lead to a network referral and make the interview go much easier.

School Job Fairs

This is similar to the school career-center jobs, with the difference being that these companies are usually looking for students who are ready to graduate. Once again, the companies will normally have a relationship developed with the school, which allows you to seek out a referral before you attend the fair.

Although you can attend the fair to just solicit information and make contacts, many applicants arrive in their best dress and with their resumes, and are ready to interview.

Major Retail Companies

Major retail companies offer the greatest opportunity to get a job in today's service-industry market. These types of businesses are always taking applications and hiring, plus it is very easy to change industries just by focusing on your competencies, as we saw in a previous chapter.

Major retail companies provide good benefits, as well as an excellent training ground (which allows you to develop your skills and then move on to whatever is your real career love). I've lost count of how many associates came to Circuit City for their first job, developed into a major talent in my store, and then left the company to follow their educational dreams and ambitions. I would guess that this scenario plays out hundreds of times in hundreds of companies around the country.

Small Businesses

Small businesses have similar benefits as the large retail companies, but many also accept paper applications, and it is sometimes possible to talk directly to the owner or general manager. Many of these companies are restaurant franchises, nonfood franchises owned by a sole proprietor, or a restaurant that is family owned.

My research shows that many of these types of businesses just want the applicant to come down to the business and talk to the hiring manager. These are the jobs that can be obtained within minutes if you can create a powerful first impression in the interview, because there is little competition and turnover is high.

State Department of Workforce Services

State workforce job listings are just about on a par with newspaper want ads when it comes to getting a job. Many of the jobs they list are manual labor, require limited competencies, and are jobs most people do not want to work at. This is where the folks on unemployment usually head to fulfill their job-search requirements.

I list the state workforce ahead of the newspaper for the simple fact that many new businesses align themselves with a state workforce when they are opening a new franchise in town. In fact, many times the interviews are held at the state office. When I opened the Utah market for Circuit City, I held all my interviews at the state workforce office because we did not even have a finished building at the time.

Sometimes these events can feel as though they're cattle calls because there can be so many people, but they can be a great way to create a powerful first impression and bypass the prequalifying of the human resource staffing companies.

Newspaper Want Ads

It is surprising that newspapers still continue to print want ads, as I believe they have outlived their usefulness. They are still beneficial as reading material (I know I used to read them over dinner on days when I was so upset with my job I just wanted to quit and go anywhere else).

The want ads are also laden with fraud, as are many Internet sites. If you look at the ads every week, it will not take long to discover that the same companies place the same ads week after week, month after month. Either their turnover is phenomenal or there is some type of fraudulent business activity going on.

Internet Job Sites

I know it seems hard to believe that I am listing the Internet as the last place to find a service-industry job. Much has been made about the Internet job banks and the convenience to not only apply for multiple jobs by sending your resume out with a click of a key, but also that companies and recruiting firms can locate you.

My experience with these options is that it is a great resource for applicants who have a great deal of experience and can contend with other highly qualified applicants, but it is of little use to young adults searching for a job in the service industry.

The Internet market has high barriers to entry in that there are thousands of candidates, all with their perfectly designed resumes listing the latest keywords to get picked up by the computers and headhunters doing the searches. This makes it very difficult for you to create a powerful first impression to get the job you want because you are being represented by that history document, your resume.

The Internet is great for allowing you to *feel* that you are doing something (sending out all those mass resumes and cover letters with the names changed), so that you go to bed with an euphoric feeling that you'll get that call in the morning from the company across the country that wants to fly you out to-morrow for an interview. I hope you do.

There are also very few desired jobs available if you live in a state that does not have many companies that advertise on the main job sites. Many of the jobs list openings in all 50 states, which should be another red flag to steer clear of them, as many times the company is a franchise in disguise and re-quires money up front.

Internet service-industry jobs are also laden with fraud and frequently are high-turnover companies that churn and burn their associates with such regularity that you will actually see the job listing as an ongoing hiring opening with no actual list-ing date. It is best to steer clear of these like the plague. Other fraudulent companies will get you to give them your personal data and then mark you as a candidate for identity theft.

Seasonal Hires

This last method to get backstage is such a little-known secret in the industry that not many people take advantage of it. Here's the absolute truth: There is no easier way to get employed by a company than as a seasonal hire.

Seasonal hiring is the bane of every management team that has to hire many associates in a matter of days. If the company's busy seasonal period takes place during Christ-mas (as mine does), it can create quite a challenge to pre-pare the store for the additional merchandise and the anticipated customer onslaught.

Throw in the need to hire and train 30 associates in a few short weeks, and it can get downright nuts. Because manage-ment knows that any hiring mistakes can and will be terminated at the end of the season, most teams will hire nearly anyone who passes the staffing company's prequalifying process and can carry on a coherent conversation in the interview.

Joe's Gem
"There is no easier way to get the job you want than as a seasonal hire."

If you can create a powerful first impression in the interview, even without a few of the competencies, you will be hired within minutes. The sad fact is that most people don't want to leave a current regular job for a temporary job that they know they are going to lose at the end of the holiday season.

I'll let you in on another secret: I never terminate a talented seasonal hire who performs above expectations. I don't care if I have a staffing opportunity for you or not; I will always make room and put you in some department. Talent is too rare and turnover is too common to let a talented associate walk out the door because your contract for hire has ended.

I currently have a sales manager who started as a seasonal associate and worked his way up. Some of Circuit City's corporate management started as seasonal associates as well. Never feel that a seasonal position is a dead end. If it is the only way you can get into a company that you want to work for, take it!

Application Strategies

We talked in an earlier chapter that the three parts of the *Preaudition* Step consisted of the application process, the resume, and telephone etiquette. We have already discussed the resume in a previous chapter, so let's now talk about the application and telephone parts of the step.

Applications are used to eliminate you from the job consideration process. You always want to create a powerful first impression with your application, whether you dropped it off in person or submitted it on a company's Website.

Did you drop off an application? Chances are you were evaluated at that time by whoever was working the frontline. Many major corporations no longer accept paper applications since moving to the electronic-based variety, but those that do will normally make an assessment of the applicant at that time.

When Circuit City accepted paper applications, my customer-service associates always gave me feedback on the applicant. Many applicants would drop off an application while shopping so it was understandable that they would not be nicely dressed, but anything weird was a definite turnoff.

The same holds true for applicants that travel in groups of friends. If you're dropping off your application with six other questionable friends, chances aren't good for a callback. Companies today are so afraid of internal theft that it's best to leave your friends at home.

Real Life

I once had a couple drop off their applications at my store some years ago. They entered the store in a passionate embrace, and continued kissing at the customer-service counter while they waited for an associate to help them. When the customer-service associate was free and finally arrived to review and accept the applications, she had to wait nearly three minutes before the kissing couple was able to break away long enough to hand her the applications. I never did discover how they would do in an interview, but it was apparent that they had a powerful first impression while in the store!

The same idea applies if you drop off the application with your boyfriend or girlfriend. A best practice would be to turn in your application alone and let your friends wait outside the business.

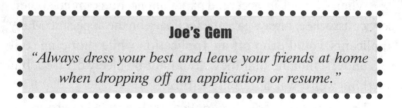

Joe's Gem

"Always dress your best and leave your friends at home when dropping off an application or resume."

Written applications must also be free from spelling errors and what I graciously call flamboyant writing. You've probably seen the type, with super-large print or all capital letters that says, "I'm important!" The same goes for its neurotic sister, where the print is so small you wonder if the applicant has any self-image at all.

Lastly, nothing is a bigger turnoff than someone who thinks filling out the application is a waste of time and doesn't bother to fill it out completely. If you're not going to waste your time, you can be sure I'm not going to waste mine. *Pass!*

I explained earlier that many companies today use electronic or Web-based applications. There are several types, but most are designed to assess certain behavioral and work-related traits. Many service-industry companies today require you to submit an application online. This type of application can take one of two forms:

- Your application is submitted through a human resource staffing company that prescreens your responses to see if any of them automatically disqualify you from the applicant pool based the hiring company's prequalifying criteria.

  ▸ This disqualification can be based on many different metrics, such as behavior profiling, previous work history, work-schedule availability, unwillingness to take a drug test, and a history of prior criminal convictions.

  ▸ This prequalifying period also tests your potential for success on the job by setting minimum behavior performance standards on the behavior tests that you take online. Most staffing companies claim to significantly reduce turnover and raise associate performance by using such standards.

  ▸ If you pass the prequalifying test, your application will be graded with your behavioral score and rated with a low, medium, or high prediction of success. The application is then sent to the store closest to your homes where it will be reviewed by a member of store management who will either contact you for an interview or reject the application.

- The application is submitted to the corporate human resource department, where it is prequalified by human resource management, and either approved or rejected.

▸ If you pass the prequalifying test, you will either be contacted by the corporate human-resource department or your application will be sent to the store closest to your home, where you will be contacted by a member of management for a possible interview.

In the *Preaudition* Step, you can be turned down here if you score below a certain level that the hiring company has determined is the minimum for their new associates based on the necessary attributes required. This part of the process is normally out of the hiring manager's hands unless an applicant is on the fence.

Joe's Gem

"Always fill out your applications completely and neatly."

It is still possible, even on a Web-based application, to not fill in pertinent areas that are needed for a hiring manager to make an educated decision as to whether or not to interview an applicant. I receive many applications a month that either have the education or job history missing. I'll sometimes excuse the absent job history if the applicant is a minor, but seldom overlook it on a more experienced applicant that should know better.

Phone Etiquette

Did you make an interview appointment over the telephone? What was your attitude like? Were you willing to accept whatever appointment was available or were you already being difficult and high-maintenance? I've had applicants say they weren't available over the course of several hours and days I was interviewing. Sometimes I wondered whether I was the one being interviewed and would have to plan around their schedule—*not*!

If the employer left a message, what did your voice mail say? Hopefully you expected the call and had a business-like recording on it. I know people who have had their friends with better-sounding voices tape their voice mail messages just to create a more powerful first impression.

Real Life

Judy, a customer-service associate of mine, called Thomas to set up an interview for a car electronics installer position. The applicant had a stable work history at a competitive business, so I anticipated meeting the individual and hopefully adding him to the team. Imagine my horror when Judy informed me that Thomas's voice mail greeting was laden with four-letter words about what he was going to do to his girlfriend that night, as well as other derogatory language towards women. Disbelieving her, I had to listen to it myself, and even I was offended (and that's saying a lot). Needless to say, the interview never took place because I would hate to steal a guy like that from the competition!

Chapter 9

Learning Your Lines:

Quick and Easy Interview Questions

The actor reprimands the writer and asks how he can ever hope to give a great performance when the writing in the script he created just sits there and is nothing more than lifeless words on a page. The writer, sensing the actor's frustration, softly says, "Yes, I created the words, but it is you who must give them life."

Similar to the actor, you must also give life to the words you say. To give an award-winning performance, you cannot read and memorize a book on how to answer 150 interview questions the night before and then expect to say the lifeless words that were written on the pages the next day.

You must infuse your voice with such passion that every word you say is filled with your character, uniqueness, and talent, leaving the interviewer with such a powerful first impression that the job you want is yours.

Be Ready for the Audible

Imagine an experienced defensive coordinator in this year's Super Bowl who has been in the league so long that he has seen every type of offensive formation. This is a coach who has intently studied the opposition, studied their game films of the entire season, and has seen tape of every play that they normally run at certain stages of the game.

He runs out onto the sidelines at game time, firm in the belief that he is as prepared as ever and ready to bring home a championship. But, because he fails to call the correct defense at the critical time, he gets beat on a trick play that sends his team to defeat. It's game over, job lost, go home.

Job interview questions are the most feared aspect of any interview, and this explains why books on answering every type of question are second only to resume books in their mass availability. Whatever question you can dream of being asked, chances are good that someone has already thought of the proper answer and you can find it in his or her book.

This works well in theory as it allows you to become exposed to and prepared for many different types of questions and scenarios. However, your experience in front of the interviewer may be an entirely different game situation than you prepared for.

What if the interviewer changes the play or the line of questioning in the interview (called the audible in football) and peppers you with questions that feel similar to trick plays because they come at inopportune times and have a different slant to them? It's game over, job lost, go home.

Practice Your Lines

There's no question that actors must flawlessly say their lines to demonstrate what ability they have. Unfortunately, you must do more than just demonstrate that you have the lines (and answers) memorized. You must call the right audible based on what play the interviewer is calling.

The fact that you have determined your motivation for the interview will allow you to speak from a position of authenticity. You should have also addressed certain deficiencies in your application style that will allow you to succinctly explain what has taken place in the past, as well as allow you to show off your current "brand." Strength comes from knowing oneself and answering in a genuine, authentic manner.

Know your weaknesses in the way a football coach knows his team's weaknesses. If a team is terrible against the run, the opposition is going to run. Similarly, if you have been changing jobs every three months, the interviewer will ask why you have been job-hopping.

If you have trained your mind to be more digital and worked through some of the processes we have covered in this book, you are ready to take the stage!

Many career book authors make a big fuss over answering the difficult questions correctly. That may be true in big business, but in the service industry, I find it is the easy questions that normally trap the applicants I interview. These are your basic, everyone-is-going-to-ask-them questions, and for these you must have a good answer. A great answer would be better, but I don't even feel that is necessary. You just don't want to give a bad answer.

I mentioned earlier that companies use resumes to look for reasons to turn you down. The same reasoning applies here. I turn more applicants down because of bad, inappropriate answers than I care to admit.

I will make you aware of the questions that trip up the applicants who have little interviewing experience. I will offer you help on what answers an interviewer wearing a uniform, rather than one wearing a suit, will be looking for.

Real Life

Mike, a Store Director friend of mine, told me about the time he interviewed Scott, who had recently been working at one of our competitors, for a product specialist position. After much of the interview had been completed, Mike covered the importance of our associates working their assigned schedule. He asked Scott what he considered a reasonable number of times for him to call in sick or be late for any reason. "Oh, 50 or 60 days a year at the very most," he said. I wonder if he still works at our competitor?

I think it is important to remember that retail-industry turnover is much higher than other industries, which is why the advice I give you may differ from what you may read in some other books. How long I envision an applicant staying with me is always foremost in my mind throughout the entire interview.

Who Are You?

Ron Fry, the dean of interviewing, states in his classic book *101 Great Answers to the Toughest Interview Questions* (highly recommended!) that the success and failure of your interview may hinge on your ability to answer the one simple question of "who are you?" I couldn't agree more.

We have worked together through the previous chapters to discover who you are and, more importantly, who you want to be. You have learned that high-octane energy, killer confidence, and engaging friendliness are the necessary ingredients in creating the powerful first impression that will allow you to get the job that you want.

You have discovered the power of using interviewer discomfort to your advantage during the interview, as well as identifying your locus of control and the necessity of driving your own bus if you want to control your own destiny.

You've identified your competencies and strengths, researched the company of your choice, and are now ready to breathe life into your lines with the skill of an award-winning actor.

Quick and Easy Questions

Can You Tell Me a Little About Yourself?

Ron Fry calls this the granddaddy of all interview questions and the one that can still make people stumble. I admit that I used to ask the question as an icebreaker as Ron states many hiring managers do. However, I have begun using it to probe the future plans of an applicant much more than discovering about his or her past.

It is a must that your high-octane energy, killer confidence, and engaging friendliness shine throughout your response. After all, you are talking about yourself! If you cannot get excited about yourself, or worse, you get apologetic that there is nothing good to say, you will not be around for long!

Always think of your brand (your features and your benefits) and of how they are applicable to the job you are trying to get. I wouldn't expect you to have the career accomplishments of an experienced manager and tell a great story if you are or were recently a student. However, this is an excellent time to talk about your brand and any accomplishments you may have had at school or on the job while tying them in to your competencies.

Mention that your leadership and teamwork helped win a sports competition, and how those attributes will help you at the company you are applying with. Perhaps your analytical and execution skills contributed to completing a great school project, and now you can see yourself utilizing those skills with this company. Maybe you have a 4.0 grade point average due to your dedication and insistence on excellence, and now you want to bring those attributes to your new company to achieve those desired goals.

What Not to Say

Although this seems to be a very innocent question, it offers much insight into your goals and motivation. Many of the applicants I interview answer this question too honestly. It is amazing how many people will nonchalantly state that they are going to work in their dad's business or will enter the police academy next month. Never offer the fact that you will be leaving in a short period of time. Only talk about the future if your prospective employer is included in it.

It also makes sense to never say anything negative about your past unless you can use the information to make a powerful first impression on the interviewer. If you recently took some time off from school or work to decide what it is you want to do in your immediate future, tie your decision into your goals and what you hope to accomplish at the company you are interviewing with.

Why Do You Want to Work Here?

We covered this topic in detail in a previous chapter. You should now have a couple of good reasons for choosing the company you are interviewing with. Remember that the more enthusiasm you can generate for the specific company, the more powerful the impression you will make. I have had applicants tell me straight up that it wouldn't matter if they were applying at my competitor. This is a sure way to find yourself out the door.

What Not to Say

The wrong reply here turns me off more than any other answer. I explained earlier that hiring managers want to hear that you are there sitting in front of them because of desire and not need. A weak answer here really stands out because, if you are not interested in the company, you are more of a flight risk to leave for a frivolous reason.

You absolutely want to refrain from mentioning any of the following reasons that may get you an automatic turndown:

- Business is close to home and it doesn't matter where you work.

- Just need a job with anyone, even one with a competitor.
- Parents are making you get a job to start earning your way.
- Need money to pay bills.
- Been out of work for a while and need to finally get back to keeping busy.

One exception to the answer of "just needing money" is when you claim to be saving for college. This answer gives the implication that you will continue working at the company even after you enter a local university. Most service-industry employers will also understand the need due to the escalating costs of an education. Tie this in with the benefit of tuition reimbursement to strengthen the answer.

Another acceptable instance is when you are seeking seasonal or temporary employment and the company knows you will be leaving and will not cause frivolous turnover.

I also will often get the "just need money" answer from applicants looking for a second job. As most people don't work a second job unless money is needed, it is both believable and entirely understandable. Just keep in mind that part-time associates with full-time jobs are flight risks who will often leave the company after a few short weeks, and the idea of probable turnover will most likely be a turnoff. However, some of my better associates in the past have been those with two jobs.

It is often best, if the full-time job is in another industry, to say that you are looking to transition into your prospective employer's industry. This indicates that if things work out you would quit your other job and move to the new one permanently.

Real Life

Steve, an applicant with a powerful first impression, was interested in working a second job at Circuit City. Steve currently worked full-time as a factory worker, and needed some extra income to help out at home. Second-job applicants are always a flight risk due to the increased pressure on both the home and social life, but I became more intrigued when Steve added that he really had a love of computers, and his dream was to quit his other job and move over to Circuit City when a full-time position opened up in the technology department. Although Steve had no experience selling computers, I knew my management team could teach him the retail side of the business and use his high-octane energy, killer confidence, and engaging friendliness to turn him into a star. In less than six months, even though it was difficult working two demanding jobs, Steve accomplished his goal of becoming a full-time player who is now making a huge impact on our technology team. Thank you, Steve, for staying with us long enough to live your dream!

Tell Me a Strength That Your Previous Employer Would Say You Had

This question drives me nuts! I cannot believe the strengths I sometimes hear. This is another opportunity for your brand to shine and for you to tie your strengths into what they can do for the company. If one of your strengths is being detailed, state how you were your manager's merchandiser of choice at your last job because you would always have all the product perfectly aligned and price-tagged, and how you could do the same for the interviewer.

If it is your engaging friendliness that is a strength, claim that you were always the one fellow associates called when there was a difficult customer to deal with, which would make you perfect candidate for the customer-service position you are applying for.

What Not to Say

A strength should be simply that: a positive attribute that can be quantified into a behavior that achieves a desired result, as illustrated in the previous examples. Never, ever say what you think is a strength but is really a weakness in disguise.

It saddens me to say that the most frequently mentioned strength that I receive from applicants is that they are a hard worker. What does that tell me? Is that a quantifiable response? *Hard worker* is a very subjective term—what is a hard worker to one person can be lazy to another. I often ask applicants what behavior I would see if I walked into his or her previous employer's business. What would they be doing? Seldom do I receive an answer that helps their cause.

Another frequently mentioned strength is that the person comes to work on time. I have never seen a job where this is optional! How can it be a strength? What does it say about an individual who admits that this is one of his or her strongest attributes? Don't you make the same mistake.

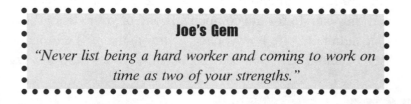

Joe's Gem

"Never list being a hard worker and coming to work on time as two of your strengths."

Tell Me a Weakness That Your Previous Employer Would Say You Had

This is similar to the previous question about your strengths. Never offer anything that can be construed as a character weakness. You must even be careful of any language that has negative meaning to it. Words such as *anal, controlling, compulsive, meticulous, talkative, perfectionist, workaholic,* and so on may seem innocent, but they can conjure up images of a person who can be difficult to work with.

The best weaknesses to mention are ones that are universal and that most people can have at one time or another. I recommend using product knowledge if you are in any industry where you must sell or interact with a product. It is easily understood that you would have liked to increase your knowledge of how a product works by learning more about features and benefits, and so on.

Another appropriate weakness would be bettering your selling skills if you did any kind of selling at all. It is acceptable for you to say that you would have liked to become a better salesperson by reading more sales psychology books, doing more role-playing, and so on, because you believe there is always room for improvement in increasing your knowledge about how to sell.

If you are applying for customer service, I would also find it acceptable if you said you wish you could have bettered your listening skills and worked on developing more empathy to better understand your customers, because every one of us can always upgrade our communication ability.

What Not to Say

We've already covered a few weaknesses not to mention, and here are a few more that are so common sense they are hard to believe, but I often hear:

- Couldn't get to work on time.
- Always tired on the job.
- Talked too much.
- Worked too slow.
- Called in sick often.
- Didn't get along with coworkers.
- Could never keep busy.
- Argued with the management.

Real Life

R.J. just left the postal service after only three months on the job and was now interviewing for a product-specialist position. I immediately became suspicious as to why R.J. would leave a job most others are trying to get into because I didn't believe the poor reason he gave me as to why he quit. The real reasons became apparent after I asked R.J. to give me one of his strengths his supervisor would say he had.

"We had a new sorter in the post office and I sorted the mail correctly. Well, most of the time," he said. I asked him what was "most of the time." Was the mail incorrectly sorted about 10 percent of the time? "Yeah, that sounds about right," R.J. said. While still considering the craziness of what he just told me was a strength, I asked him what he thought his supervisor would say

---

> was a weakness. R.J. didn't hesitate to say that "it was probably coming to work tired every day since the job started early in the morning." That was the end of that interview. Imagine my cash drawers coming up 10 percent short every day!

What Was It You Liked Most About Your Last Job?

It should be apparent about now that every question, although asked for different reasons, is answered in the same manner. That is, you answer the question in a way that reflects your brand's features and benefits.

You must answer this question in a way that shows whatever you liked about your last job is the same attribute that will be needed for the prospective job. If your last job was as a temporary retail hire during the Christmas season, and you are applying at a busy retail store as a merchandiser, you might say that you enjoyed the fast pace as the constant advertising deadlines challenged your merchandise execution skills.

If you worked at a restaurant and are applying at another restaurant, you could say that you enjoyed using the slow periods to spend time getting to know and engage with your customers to help improve add-on sales.

What Not to Say

Don't say that the best part of your last job was the people unless you can describe how great the teamwork was and how everyone worked together for a common goal. If you allow the interviewer to believe that it was just a party atmosphere where everyone hung out together, it will do nothing to increase your chances to get the job that you want. Other inappropriate answers would be the free food, discounted drinks, and so on.

What Was It You Liked Least About Your Last Job?

This is similar to the what did you enjoy most question, although it is filled with more dangerous terrain. The best way to answer this question is to use a weakness inherent in the previous business that did not utilize a strength of yours that the new position will. For example, you did a great deal of selling over the phone rather than the face-to-face selling that the new job will require, which better utilizes your communication style. Or, the previous restaurant business was slow and did not fully utilize your multitasking skills the way the new job at the busy restaurant would.

What Not to Say

Be absolutely careful not to say you disliked anything that you will encounter if hired for the prospective job. I sometimes get applicants who say their customers were the thing they liked least. Unless you can prove how your customers were unique, that answer will literally disqualify you from getting any job that deals with customers, which are the majority of the positions in the service industry.

Never, ever say the management! Unless you can justify the answer by saying there were morale or hostile work environment issues, it always comes off that you are someone who has trouble with authority. Few hiring managers will take a chance on someone who may turn out to be a problem.

Why Did You Leave/Are You Leaving Your Last/Current Job?

This question is asked to probe whether or not you are changing jobs for better opportunities or just running away from a job where you are being disciplined or on the verge of being terminated.

I often get applicants who want to work at Circuit City to get out of the fast-food industry, which is quite often a teen's first job. It is not uncommon for me to see interviewees with three or four fast-food jobs over a six month period, especially when summer employment stints are added in.

It is imperative that you convince the interviewer that you left your previous positions to either change industries or to get more pay and responsibility. I often discover, when probing deeper, that schedule conflicts are a big reason why young adults frequently jump jobs. Conflicts over school, extracurricular activities, and social life make up a large part of the job obstacles.

This is a red flag to the interviewer that you may be a high-maintenance hire unless you can demonstrate that the issue that caused the conflict is no longer applicable, such as you recently graduated from high school and no longer have football practice.

Also, having a great reason as to why you are interviewing for the present position adds some credibility here. If you have demonstrated that you researched the company and this is the job that you see yourself working at while in school, it may help you calm any fears the interviewer may have.

Where Do You See Yourself in Five Years?

I alluded to the fact earlier that most people don't even know where they see themselves tomorrow, let alone in five years.

However, you should be better prepared to answer this question now that you have a digital mind and can see your future more clearly.

Ron Fry states that this question is used to see if your goals and the company goals are compatible. Again, the turnover rate in the service industry must be taken into consideration. Most interviewers would be thrilled to hire a student who will be with the company for at least two years while he or she finishes college, as this would allow more than enough time to develop the applicant into a lead or supervisor.

Young adults who enter the service industry seldom expect to spend the rest of their working days there. Most see the position as a rest stop on the way to a "real" job, although what that job actually is often remains unclear.

Because of this, I seldom get an answer from an applicant that he or she sees himself with my company in five years. Many associates in retail management are there because they were promoted at a young age due to their superior abilities, and they then remained with the company due to an income level that is difficult to find in another industry that utilizes similar competencies.

What Not to Say

The worst way to answer this question, of course, would be to demonstrate that you haven't thought about your future at all.

Tell Me About a Time When You Had to Deal With an Angry Customer

This is a question you should expect if your job would entail dealing with the customer in any capacity, but especially in customer service. The interviewer is looking to see how you handle customers under stress, what your empathy and communication skills are like, and whether or not you can solve the issue without involving a manager.

Always give an example that shows how you listened to the customer and understood their issue. I look for critical-thinking skills here, and whether or not you can balance the needs of the business with those of the customer.

If a customer special-ordered a hamburger and discovered it was incorrectly made upon arriving home, how would you handle the situation when they came back into the store?

The best way to answer would be that you apologized for the poor service and experience, and then offered a solution to resolve the issue, such as giving the customer his or her money back, or perhaps a gift card for his or her time and gas expense.

Dress Rehearsal

You've now learned your lines and are ready for the dress rehearsal! Let's see how dressing for success can help create a powerful first impression so you can increase your chance to get the job you want.

Chapter 10

Leave Your
Nose Ring at Home:

Dressing
for Success

The actor, arriving in torn jeans, t-shirt, and tennis shoes, stepped out of wardrobe totally transformed and dressed so accurately for the time period that it was difficult to imagine anyone else playing the part.

I don't know why, but this topic seems to upset service-industry managers more than any other part of the hiring process. It seems as if every manager I talk to has several stories about how an applicant arrived for an interview totally dressed inappropriately.

I asked myself why this would happen. Why would an applicant who has gotten to this point in the process show up for the interview as if he or she had just fallen out of bed, which by the way is one of the stories I often hear.

The way you present yourself for the interview falls under the *audition* step, and is just as important as your greeting. This is definitely not the time to fall victim to a wardrobe malfunction. You cannot get the job you want by creating a powerful first impression if you look as though you slept in your clothes, smell as though you didn't take a bath, have hair that appears to not have been washed in days, and have a tongue ring that goes click, click, click. Unless, of course, you were applying at a business that was looking for someone exactly like you.

Times Have Changed

I still talk to managers who will not interview anyone wearing tennis shoes or jeans, or who doesn't have his or her shirt tucked. I have to question their thinking to eliminate every candidate who shows up and fails to meet their dress expectations (although I do not recommend arriving in that condition).

I have to admit that for many years I was exactly the same. I felt that the candidates were being disrespectful to me whenever they showed up dressed as if they were ready to go to the movies.

Times have changed.

Real Life

Brenda showed up for an interview dressed in a bowling outfit from head to toe. I attempted to catch my breath after seeing the sight, and then decided to continue with the interview and meet with her in my office. "I'm sorry I'm dressed like this," she said. "My league starts shortly, so I came ready to play." I asked her how long she had until her first game (I seem to get bowler applicants coming into my store). Brenda glanced at her watch and stated that, "It started three minutes ago." I believe she was out in time to catch the fifth frame.

Although a business-like appearance is still important to me, and is definitely needed to create a powerful first impression, talent in the retail industry is so thin that I cannot overlook an applicant simply because he or she is not wearing the proper clothes. I have hired too many talented associates that other managers would have immediately turned down because they didn't wear the right shoes, the right pants, the right shirt. Ridiculous.

We are all a team in my store, and when customers walk in and see everyone in uniform, they have no idea who applied in tennis shoes or blue jeans. They just know if they have been given great customer service or not.

Although I admit that applicants on the extreme end might not get hired even if they came dressed in a suit, there are those who were terrible dressers when they applied, but do a great job for me in the store.

Applicant dress standards have also relaxed over the years—only the hiring managers haven't relaxed. When the majority of young adult applicants think it is okay to wear tennis shoes to a job or have their shirt hanging outside their pants, more is going on than just bad judgment.

Dressing for Success

Most people would think it is common sense for you to know how to dress for an interview, but in the service industry, dressing for success is in very short supply. Styles of dress have changed so quickly and dramatically that what was once acceptable no longer is, and vice versa.

Real Life

I interviewed Connie for a technology-product specialist position. Connie was a sharp applicant who had the high-octane energy, killer confidence, and engaging friendliness needed to make her successful. Connie certainly created a powerful first impression when we greeted each other: at least until she said hello, and I saw the huge tongue ring shining brightly under the fluorescent lights. "Tell me a little about yourself," I asked. "I'm attending click, click, click," she said, "and I hope to click, click, and click before the end of the year." Needless to say, I clicked her right out of the store.

A good idea is to go to the business you are hoping to get the job at and see what the style of dress everyone is wearing. If it is in the service industry, chances are good that the associates may be wearing a uniform. Some stores, such as the mass-market retail clubs, wear jeans and t-shirts and what-ever else they like (or so it seems).

Most career counselors would recommend dressing one level up for the job you want. Some others warn against over-dressing, as it can appear you are out of touch in the other direction.

I'm going to give you my secret to creating a powerful first impression and getting hired quickly in the service industry if you are male: Always wear a tie if you want to double your chances! The number of applicants who show up in a tie is practically zero, so you will surely stand out.

As old-fashioned as it sounds, there is still something about a young adult who arrives for an interview in a tie that says he is ready to work. I'll tend to overlook his wrinkled shirt if it looks as though he made an effort to impress me.

Dressing for Success Hotspots

Let's take a look at some of the hotspots in dressing suc-cessfully for a service-industry job interview. I've broken down dressing for interview success into the following areas:

- ◆ **Clothing.** Clothing encompasses your shirt, pants, dresses, sweater, suit, tie, and so on. As I stated earlier, men wearing a tie double their chances to get the job. I recommend wearing casual busi-ness pants, such as Dockers, along with a col-lared shirt to the interview. And yes, make sure the shirt is tucked in. Nowadays, it is acceptable for a woman to wear a dress or slacks. Pair your dress slacks with a nice top (nothing too reveal-ing or tight). Of course, it should go without saying that the clothes should be neatly pressed. (You wouldn't believe how many wrinkled shirts I see.)

◆ **Shoes.** Your shoes should always be clean and polished. You should avoid wearing tennis shoes, although there are many nice ones that give the appearance of being appropriate. Refrain from wearing any type of weird shoes or boots unless you live in a town where it is common, such as wearing cowboy boots in a western town.

◆ **Jewelry.** Should you or should you not leave your nose ring at home? Although I allow my associates to wear small nose rings in the store, I recommend taking them out for the interview. This also goes for any other kind of facial piercing, including the *click, click* tongue ring. Any kind of weird, flamboyant jewelry should also be removed.

◆ **Odors.** Odors are deal-breakers because hiring managers cannot tell if it is an isolated occurrence or general bad hygiene (and they aren't willing to take a chance). I have worked with some associates who smell as though they haven't showered for weeks—even though they did that morning (or so they told me). Some people just have clothes that smell all the time, despite many washings. Also, refrain from eating any food before your interview that might make your breath stand out. Your perfume or aftershave should also be subtle and not stand out so the whole company can smell it.

Real Life

I was interviewing Lisa, a very nice applicant who desired to work for Circuit City as a merchandise product specialist, in a small sales office because my office was being used at the time. The interview with Lisa was going very well as she created a powerful first impression upon our greeting, and she had several of the competencies we were looking for. There was only one thing wrong about her: She had the strongest perfume odor I had smelled on anyone. Ever! Because I was stuck in the small confines of the office with that penetrating smell, my eyes began to water after about three minutes into the interview. Then my coughing fit started, and didn't end for several minutes afterward (which was more than enough time for my sales manager escort her out of the office—and store). I wonder if she ever wore that fragrance again?

- **Hair.** This seems to affect the guys more than it does the girls, and I still can't figure out why. I have seen some men with the weirdest hair—as if they slept on it standing on their head. I have also asked a few men to cut their hair before they were hired. I recommend having your hair business length, but of course the acceptable length may differ depending on the type of company you are applying to.

- **Weird stuff.** What can this possibly be? This is the catch-all for anything that does not fit into one of the preceding categories, such as offensive tattoos, weird accessories, or inappropriate flourishes such as glittery or heavy makeup. I've also interviewed people with strange glasses that I first thought were part of some type of clown costume. I suppose this is where I can put applicants wearing bowling outfits or any other sports outfits. If you decided to advertise on your forehead, that would probably go here also. I'm all for being different and original, but you might need to tone things down for your interview. Eliminate anything that may distract the interviewer from your winning personality!

It's Showtime

The time has finally come! You have come this far and now you are ready to go into the interview and show your stuff. Now that you have your wardrobe under control, you can be sure you will make a powerful first impression rather than a powerful first distraction!

Chapter 11

Curtain's Up:

Getting the Part at the Audition

The director shouts, "Action!" and the actor immediately goes into character. It doesn't matter at that point that he is a struggling artist with a few cents in his pocket, his phone disconnected, and no money to pay the rent. He is, for that moment, Hamlet.

Break a leg, baby. This ain't no cold read at a cattle call! This is the real deal. You know the script, you know your motivation, now you just have to go out and get the part. Many actors have missed out on a career just because they flubbed their lines under the pressure!

Body Talk

We've already covered what the body-talk step consisted of, but let's go over it in detail as you are now at the company of your choice awaiting your interview. Remember, you are under scrutiny from the moment you check in to announce your arrival to the time the interview is completed. Controlling what your body says is just as important as controlling what you say in order to create a powerful first impression.

There are many managers who will turn you down for any of the following mistakes rather than continue on with the interview:

- ◆ **Tardiness.** Being on time for an interview is a given that shouldn't have to be said. I recommend arriving no more than 10 minutes early for the interview. I have applicants who sometimes arrive 30 minutes or more before their scheduled interview time. This is far too early, especially when I can seldom accommodate their unexpected arrival due to business needs. This also makes it look like you have nothing better to do, which is never a good sign.

Real Life

Lew, a Store Director friend of mine, told me about the time he was scheduled for a 3 p.m. interview with James, a product specialist applicant. After waiting 20 minutes for him to show, Lew had him turned down as a no-show. Imagine his surprise at 4:15 p.m. when James, who was now more than an hour late, showed up and *begged Lew to still give him the interview. Lew reluctantly agreed as James was one of his customers and he still wanted to be on good terms with him. After a brief moment of pleasantries, Lew asked James why he had been over an hour late for the interview. "My mom forgot to wake me up," he said. Last I heard he still wasn't working for Lew.*

- ◆ **Rudeness to associates.** Never become rude to any associate for any reason while you are on your interview visit. Of course, this is good advice at any time, but negative behavior will stand out much more when you are under consideration for hire. I can guarantee that word will get to the hiring manager and your interview will be finished before you get your chance to shine. I have seen applicants make sexual comments to opposite sex associates while they were waiting—not the best way to start off the interview.

- ◆ **Agitated due to waiting for interviewer.** I spoke about this earlier that some managers will purposely make you wait to see how you handle the stress. Most businesses today run on lean business models that do not allow for overstaffing, thus requiring associates to multitask and execute more than ever before. If it appears you cannot handle the stress, you will be a quick turndown.

Real Life

Ricky, an applicant for a bus-boy position, was waiting for his interview with the restaurant general manager, who was running several minutes late. The assistant manager finally arrived in his place, apologized for the delay, and asked Ricky if he wanted to have a beer while he waited a few more minutes. "Sure. Hey, that's pretty cool," Ricky said as the assistant manager poured a cold one. After another 20 minutes passed and the general manager never arrived, Ricky went to track him down, finally locating him near the kitchen door. Ricky questioned him about what was going on with the interview. "Are you nuts? You accept a beer on an interview and you expect us to hire you?" the general manager replied. "Don't let the door hit you on the way out." I never heard if it did.

- ◆ **Improperly dressed.** We covered this in a previous chapter. Use common sense and dress appropriately.
- ◆ **Extremely poor nonverbal communication skills.** You must make a powerful first impression from the moment you enter the business. Making grunts about being there for a job to the associate who greets you is not going to win any points with the interviewer. Be sure to make eye contact with your interviewer—and use your most powerful weapon: your smile!

Joe's Gem

"Always be sure to shut your cell phone off before interviewing."

- **Extreme nervousness.** You must take care that you are not overly nervous or anxious when you are waiting for the hiring manager, or during the interview itself. Negative mannerisms include extreme shaking of your leg or foot, pacing back and forth, swiveling in your chair, biting your lips and fingernails, and playing with your ring, hair, or some other object. Patiently sitting tall in your seat is the proper way to wait for your interviewer to arrive.

- **Weird stuff.** What can this possibly be? Similar to the previous chapter, this is a catch-all where we put crazy things such as not shutting your cell phone off, slouching in your seat, and performing nervous twitches with your eyes, mouth, or whatever. Chewing gum goes under weird rather than nervousness because, well, what else can you call it when an applicant pops a bubble in the middle of an interview?

Real Life

I was in the middle of interviewing Sam, a warehouse product specialist applicant, when his cell phone loudly went off in the middle of questioning. Did Sam apologize

> *and discretely turn his phone off? "What's up, Cuz?" he answered. I sat there in shock, waiting for what seemed to be several minutes as he carried on his conversation about that night's party at the local college. "Really?" Sam continued, "I'd better go then." Sam got out of his chair, stated that he had to leave, and asked if we could finish another time. You probably won't be surprised to hear that we didn't.*

The time has come to greet the interviewer. This is not a moment to get timid. There are two things you must *absolutely* do at this point, because this is where your powerful first impression with the interviewer begins:

- Flash a big, genuine smile.
- Give a firm handshake.

Smile

Nothing, and I mean nothing, sets the tone for my interviews the way a big, genuine smile does. I *immediately* begin thinking that the applicant looks encouraging and I am anxious to discover more about him or her in order to add them to the team.

A big smile accomplishes three things. It immediately gives the impression of high-octane energy because the act of smiling alone forces you to use energy. Have you ever met anyone who barely cracked a smile when introduced to you? What kind of energy did you feel from him or her? Doesn't that kind of person always seem to be so low on energy that it appears to be difficult to even walk around and breathe?

Second, it forces you to make good eye contact. It's difficult to flash a big smile and look off to the side (and it doesn't make any sense).

Lastly, a big smile is also being engagingly friendly by extending an invitation to the interviewer to learn more about you. This gives the impression that you have nothing to hide and you're willing to share a part of your life for a short time.

Handshake

Psychologists have believed for years that a person's handshake is a reflection of their personality, and that it influences our first impressions of the person whose hand we are shaking. A firm handshake has been shown in studies to be related to extraversion and emotional expressiveness, and negatively to shyness and neuroticism.

Have you ever shaken the hand of someone who barely put it into your hand? What did you think of them? Did you want to learn more about that person? It's difficult not to think that the rest of the personality is going to be just as meek.

A firm handshake is your killer confidence! It says to the interviewer, "Let's go, I'm ready."

Cute Meet

You have only seconds to develop your cute meet and verbalize an observation that will start your audition in a memorable way as you enter the interviewer's office and take your seat.

Don't panic if you cannot think of anything original! Talk about the weather if you are in the middle of a storm, that you noticed how busy the store was while you were waiting, or that the associate you interacted with had such a great, professional attitude. Anything that's a good icebreaker and requires the interviewer to give a response.

I remember an interview I once had for a sales position where I walked into the interviewer's office and saw nothing but Michael Jordan memorabilia covering the total room. I mean, the stuff was *everywhere*! I immediately knew that not only was Michael Jordan important in his life as a basketball fan, but that he idolized who he was.

I mentioned to the interviewer that, being from Chicago myself, I also admired Jordan. Not so much for his playing ability, however, but because he never rested on his laurels, and he came out night after night and put everything he had on the line. That is what made him a winner, and that same type of attitude is what I would bring to my interviewer's team to help make his department a winner.

The cute meet must have worked because I was offered the job in less than 10 minutes.

Stage Fright

Stage fright is normal at this time. Sure, you have some performance anxiety, but we've already discussed that it's healthy to experience a little at this time. What you don't want to do is get into a situation where you panic so much that you begin to flub your lines, for if you do, the audition is done and you can kiss your part goodbye.

No matter your situation, no matter your desperation, you must never have such a fear that it will become debilitating in the interview. Never fear the thought of not getting the job: It will always affect your performance.

If you truly believe that failure is not an option, you will play your best role and give your best performance. If it's enough to get you the job, great. If not, perhaps there will be another audition tomorrow. Sometimes great things take time. Never panic.

Show Them the "It" Factor

I described this step of the interview earlier as the *audition* simply because that is how you must feel. You are making the position yours in such a way that the interviewer cannot see anyone else but you in the role of the job. Your killer confidence must shine here, and you must not feel that you are under pressure.

Show the interviewer your "it" factor (your brand) and focus on your features and benefits. You must have the confidence that, even if there will be 100 more interviews after you, it is your uniqueness that will get you the part and cause the interviewer to look for more reasons to hire you.

You must remember that you will have already created a powerful first impression, so the effect of that experience will definitely be on your side. The interviewer *is looking for more reasons to hire you*, so that is what you must give him. He or she is *expecting* the "it" factor (your brand) give it to them!

The Innerview

Most hiring managers pride themselves on being able to spot what I call the interviewing phony. We have all probably played the part once or twice in our job search career. A slick, polished performance saying the answers we believe the interviewer wants to hear even if it means lying to ourselves to get the job.

This applicant still shows his or her face in my office at least a few times a month. Skilled interviewers want to be dazzled. They have probably spent hours looking at other characters who have said the lines they thought the interviewer wanted said.

I have spoken much about actors and used the acting analogy quite often. However, have I ever once said for you to "act" in the interview? Have I ever said for you to pretend to be someone you are not?

Now, I have a confession to make. All of that was just to get you to the audition to face your fears. The truth is that once you are in the interview sitting across from the person who can give you the job, the acting must stop.

You must realize at this time that you are in an *innerview* and not an *interview*, and if thought of in this manner, it should be relatively easy for you to focus on exactly what you need to say so that the inner you shines. The innerviewer only cares about what you can do for his or her business, and whether or not you will fit in as an associate. He or she needs to experience the real deal.

The great psychologist Carl Rogers exhibited in his person-centered therapy a quality called genuineness. Rogers believed that when a therapist dropped their facade and genuinely expressed his true feelings, his clients increased their self-understanding and self-acceptance. *You* must drop your facade and be genuine in the innerview.

Henry James, the literary scholar, had what he called his theory of illumination. James's theory was that whenever the main character in a story would interact with another character, they would each share some previously unknown aspect of their life with each other.

I recommend that you do the same every time a question is asked. Each instance is an opportunity for you to demonstrate your brand, share an unknown strength and competency by using a PAR, and talk about your features and benefits to the innerviewer.

Voice-Over

Have you ever met a member of the opposite sex for the first time and said or done something that embarrassed you enough that you would have liked to take it back? Who was that little voice in your head that made you aware of your act by saying, "That was stupid." Or, how about the voice that questions your character and asks, "Are you going to ask her out or are you just going to sit there like a loser?"

Screenwriters use a similar device called a "voice-over" in their screenplays when they require a narrator to talk over the action to set the opening of a story or explain what is going on, such as Kevin Costner's character in *Dances with Wolves*.

Many of us, in stressful situations, sometimes talk to ourselves as if we are a person in need. It oftentimes seems as if we have an imaginary friend in our head who shows his or her voice when we need an explanation of what is going on. I would often listen to the voice in my head while up at the plate or on the mound in the middle of a close baseball game to convince myself that I was better than the opponent and had what it took to win.

When under stress in the interview, you may resort to using voice-over to calm yourself or give yourself direction. If you question the path the interview is taking and require a pep talk to get back on track, you'll begin hearing from your imaginary friend again saying things such as, "That was a stupid answer you just gave," or, "You might as well quit now, you've already lost the job."

You must refrain from using your own voice-over during an the interview. It is nearly impossible to carry on a conversation with yourself and be accepted as genuine by the interviewer at the same time because your listening skills are often compromised.

I have been in interviews myself where I would have an internal dialogue asking how I was doing and where was the interviewer going with his questions. The end result was that I always appeared preoccupied and never got the job.

Questions to Ask

Learning what questions to ask is just as important as knowing how to answer the questions. Ron Fry, in his book *101 Smart Questions to Ask On Your Interview*, believes that this last phase of the interview is perhaps the most important because failing to prepare properly can undue all the good you have earned up until this point.

This is your moment to show off the depth of the research you did in the Web wizard step and remind the interviewer how perfect you are for the job. If you came across some interesting business information that you wanted to ask about, this is the time to do it.

I always appreciate it when I am asked intelligent questions because it gives me a chance to talk about how great my company is. Many applicants ask how long I have been with the company or do I like working there, which always says to me that the person is not just out looking for any job.

Another good question to ask is what your responsibilities and expectations would be for the job you are applying for, and how would your performance be evaluated.

If you have not covered the topic earlier, it can be beneficial to inquire about the company's career path for both management and nonmanagement positions. This shows that you are interested in being developed and growing as an associate.

Ending the Interview

It is probable that you may be asked for a second interview, as most companies will have at least two managers interview you for a position. I always have the applicant's potential department manager interview the candidate because they will be the manager responsible for the associate's performance.

If you are not set up for a second interview, you should always have an idea of when or if you are going to be contacted about the hiring decision.

Many companies have eliminated notifying every candidate of its decision due to the cost savings and will often just call you if you are chosen for the position. Some companies may still mail what's called a turn-down card, which is basically a form letter stating that you did not get the position.

I know it can sometimes seem a little impersonal to not get a call back, but some companies interview such a large number of candidates that it does not make good business sense to do it.

Lastly, many books recommend sending a personal thank-you letter to the interviewer for being given the opportunity to interview. I believe this is effective for positions where the competition is fierce, such as in an industry that has a high barrier to entry.

I don't believe this is necessary in the service industry for the simple fact that most hiring decisions will not take place based on a thank-you note. The truth is that the decision on whether to hire you or not will probably be made before you even leave. Also, most service-industry managers are so busy that they would probably give the note no more than a passing glance.

You're Hired

Hopefully, you get the phone call you've been waiting for saying that you have the job! It's time to start planning you next career move—your promotion!

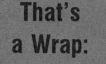

Chapter 12

That's a Wrap:

After You're on the Payroll

The actor takes his bow—he's finally made it, he's done his greatest work, and he now hears the applause that he's dreamed about for years—then the director asks him, "What's next?"

You have just been hired for the job you always wanted—congratulations! You've come a long way from where you once started. Hopefully, you are not the same person you were when we began our journey many pages ago.

You now know how to create such a powerful first impression that you will be able to use it for the rest of your years, and in more ways than just for your career. Your high-octane energy, killer confidence, and engaging friendliness will work in conjunction with your digital mind to ensure that you progress in whatever career you choose.

Most importantly, you are now the driver of your own bus, and your own destiny. You will steer it in whatever direction you please, to attain any dreams you desire. And, if you want to take a detour off road for a short time and see where that gets you, then by all means do it.

Your First Day

Your first day on the job is always one that is difficult in that everything is new and unfamiliar. The building is new, the job expectations are new, and, more importantly, so are the people. It is sometimes challenging to meet many new people and be able to remember their faces and names, but always create a powerful first impression with every single person you meet and soon they will seem to be old friends.

Remember what you learned about fear and how your killer confidence can hammer it down whenever it shows its ugly face. It is normal to feel apprehensive when you first begin a new job. Enjoy it!

Do your very best to show your management team that they made the correct decision to hire you, and that you are a quick learner and can do the job better than anyone else. Don't be a flameout that tears it up for a few weeks to stand above the crowd, and then pull back on your performance because nobody cares and that's what all the other associates do. Always insist on excellence of yourself and do your very best. People *will* begin to notice and you will start to receive recognition.

What's Next

It is mandatory in the high-turnover service industry that you prepare yourself for the next step. Promotions come quickly, and they come to those who are prepared.

Although it will take time for you to learn how to properly do your current job, there are always opportunities for those who are willing to take on extra tasks and extra responsibilities. Never turn down any assignment that can lead to developing more competencies and give you the possibility to achieve more success.

I have promoted associates just days after they were hired when I've lost a pivotal person due to attrition or promotion. I never consider how little time the person has been with me. It only matters whether they have the competencies to learn and do the job.

Needed Competencies

If you are to quickly move up the ranks in your company, it is necessary to gather the required competencies for your future position. Always monitor the position above yours that you desire and try to determine what competencies are required by the current person in that role.

It would be of great benefit for you to volunteer your services to your supervisor or manager to gain experience in jobs other than your own. This will help develop skills that will be required in future months and years.

It is without question that the one competency you must obtain and that others will be looking for you to have before promoting you is leadership. I'm not talking about the kind of leadership that is needed to manage an entire store, but the style of leadership required to manage and organize small groups of people who can use teamwork to achieve results.

I recommend keeping a log book of some kind to track your PARs as they arise. Every time you perform a task where you must lead others into accomplishing some goal is an opportunity for you to record the problem, action, and result (PAR).

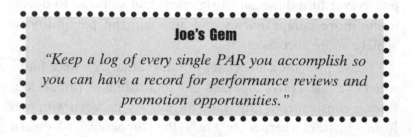

Joe's Gem

"Keep a log of every single PAR you accomplish so you can have a record for performance reviews and promotion opportunities."

PARs are also great to use when you are getting a performance review or evaluation. Instead of saying how valuable you are and what work you did all year, you can give valid, detailed accomplishments. Remember to always talk about your brand as well as your features and benefits.

Another required competency to lead a team is execution skill. If you are not effective at execution, it will be difficult for you to get results no matter how good a leader you are. Always make every attempt to develop your execution skills whenever possible.

Seasonal Associates

If you are a seasonal associate hoping to stay on, pay attention to everything I have said in the preceding paragraphs. Although managers have to work with different staffing models, it is hard for me to imagine any manager terminating a top performer just because the season ends, knowing he or she may need another person tomorrow due to attrition.

Seasonal associates are special people. It is not easy to get hired in the absolute beginning of the holiday season, get thrown on the sales floor with little training, and then expect to perform as a seasoned veteran.

However, this is what makes it so easy for you to stand out, simply because the expectations are so low. The seasonal associate who does outperform his regular peers will stand out for all to see and will most likely be asked to stay on as a regular associate.

Good luck in your future. I wish you the best that the world has to offer. I believe I have given you a good head start, and it is now up to you to keep your lead forever. Keep chasing your dreams and you will get the life you want by creating a powerful first impression! I look forward to the day that our big yellow school buses cross paths!

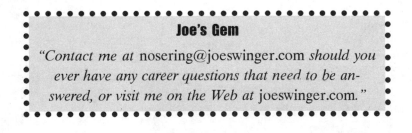

Joe's Gem

"Contact me at nosering@joeswinger.com *should you ever have any career questions that need to be answered, or visit me on the Web at* joeswinger.com.*"*

Recommended Reading

Allen, Robert. *Multiple Streams of Income*. Hoboken, N.J.: John Wiley & Sons, Inc., 2004.

Allen, Robert, and Mark Victor Hansen. *Cracking the Millionaire Code: Your Key to Enlightened Wealth*. New York: Harmony Books, 2005.

Allen, Robert, and Mark Victor Hansen. *The One Minute Millionaire: The Enlightened Way to Wealth*. New York: Harmony Books, 2002.

Canfield, Jack, and Mark Hansen. *The Aladdin Factor*. New York: The Berkley Publishing Group, 1995.

Canfield, Jack, Mark Hansen, and Les Hewitt. *The Power of Focus: How to Hit Your Business, Personal and Financial Targets with Absolute Certainty*. Deerfield Beach, Fla.: Health Communications, 2000.

Canfield, Jack, and Janet Switzer. *The Success Principles: How to Get From Where You are to Where You Want to Be*. New York: HarperCollins Publishers Inc., 2005.

Cialdini, Robert. *Influence: the Psychology of Persuasion*. New York: William Morrow and Company, Inc., 1993.

Eker, T. Harv. *Secrets of the Millionaire Mind: Mastering the Inner Game of Wealth*. New York: HarperCollins Publishers Inc., 2005.

Finley, Guy. *The Secret Way of Wonder: Insights from the Silence*. St. Paul, Minn.: Llewellyn Publications, 1992.

Medley, Anthony. *Sweaty Palms: the Neglected Art of Being Interviewed*. New York: Time Warner Book Group, 2005.

Mortensen, Kurt. *Maximum Influence: The 12 Universal Laws of Power Persuasion*. New York: AMACOM, 2004.

Bibliography

Ambady, Nalini, and Robert Rosenthal. "Half a Minute: Predicting Teacher Evaluations From Thin Slices of Nonverbal Behavior and Physical Attractiveness." *Journal of Personality and Social Psychology* 64 (1993): 431–441.

———. "On Judging and being Judged Accurately in Zero-Acquaintance Situations." *Journal of Personality and Social Psychology* 69 (1995): 518–529.

Bermont, Todd. *10 Insider Secrets to a Winning Job Search.* Franklin Lakes, N.J.: Career Press, 2004.

Bolles, Richard Nelson. *What Color Is Your Parachute?* Berkeley: Ten Speed Press, 2006.

Buckingham, Marcus, and Donald Clifton. *Now, Discover Your Strengths*. New York: The Free Press, 2001.

Canfield, Jack, and Janet Switzer. *The Success Principles*. New York: Collins, 2005.

Chaplin, et al. "Handshaking, Gender, Personality, and First Impressions." *Journal of Personality and Psychology* 79 (2000): 110–117.

David, et al. "Consensus at Zero Acquaintance: Replication, Behavioral Cues, and Stability." *Journal of Personality and Social Psychology* 62 (1992): 88–97.

Festinger, Leon. *A Theory of Cognitive Dissonance*. Stanford, California: Stanford University Press, 1957.

Fry, Ron. *101 Great Answers to the Toughest Interview Questions*. Clifton Park, New York: Thomson Delmar Learning, 2000.

————. *101 Smart Questions to Ask on Your Interview*. Clifton Park, New York: Thomson Delmar Learning, 2006.

Hansen, Mark, and Robert Allen. *The One-Minute Millionaire*. New York: Harmony, 2002.

Heatherton, Todd, and Janet Polivy. "Development and Validation of a Scale for Measuring State Self-Esteem." *Journal of Personality and Social Psychology* 60 (1991): 895–910.

Kenny, David, and Linda Albright. "Accuracy in Interpersonal Perception: a Social Relations Analysis." *Psychological Bulletin* 102 (1987): 390-402.

Kessler, Robin, and Linda Strasburg. *Competency-Based Resumes*. Franklin Lakes, New Jersey: Career Press, 2005.

Levesque, Maurice J., and David Kenny. "Accuracy of Behavioral Predictions at Zero Acquaintance: a Social Relations Analysis." *Journal of Personality and Social Psychology* 65 (1993): 1178–1187.

Mortensen, Kurt. *Maximum Influence*. New York: American Management Association, 2004.

Noe, John R. *Peak Performance Principles for High Achievers*. New York: Berkley Publishing Group, 1986.

Nordstrom, et al. "First Impressions Versus Good Impressions: The Effect of Self-Regulation on Interview Evaluations." *The Journal of Psychology* 132 (1998): 477–491.

Reed, Jon, and Rachel Myers. *Resumes From Hell*. Northampton, Massachusetts: Ecruiting Alternatives Inc., 2004.

Rotter, J. B. "Generalized Expectancies for Internal Versus External Control of Reinforcement." *Psychological Monographs* 80 (1966): 69.

Ryan, Robin. *Soaring on Your Strengths*. New York: Penguin, 2005.

Index

About the Author

Joe Swinger is director of the personal-development company in2momentum, where he helps others achieve their dreams by maximizing their moments. Swinger believes that it only takes a moment to change a life. He has spent the last 20 years in retail management, most recently as a Store Director with Circuit City, where he has developed numerous successful business leaders while achieving extraordinary results. *Leave Your Nose Ring at Home* is based on the thousands of interviews he has performed throughout his retail career. He has also spent many years writing screenplays and has received both the UCLA Diane Thomas and Disney Fellowship screenwriting awards.

Swinger received his Bachelor of Arts degree in psychology from the University of California, Los Angeles, and his Master of Arts degree in psychology from Pepperdine University. He also has a Master of Science degree in Business Administration from Westminster College in Salt Lake City.

Swinger speaks on a broad spectrum of business and human development topics to both students and business professionals. He is available for training and consultation on how to create a powerful first impression in an interview. Swinger lives in Salt Lake City, Utah, with his wife and twin sons. He can be reached at *nosering@joeswinger.com* and can also be visited on the Web at *joeswinger.com*.